Angelo Martins Junior

Lives in Motion – notebooks of an immigrant in London

Images by Yanni Eleftherakos

ISBN 978-8792632-36-4
Photography: Visual Ethnographer, Yanni Eleftherakos © 2014
Cover design & Layout by Design Amorandi

Published by
Whyte Tracks
Møllehavegård
3200 Helsinge
Denmark
www.whytetracks.eu.com

CONTENTS

DEDICATION

To my parents, Angelo Martins and Maria Leonilda F. Martins,
for all the love, care and affection.

To Goldsmiths, University of London,
for the guidance and support in making this book possible.

INTRODUCTION

In the last three decades, improvements in communication and transport systems have facilitated the development and management of multiple forms of interconnection of networking activities across the world. Intense 'mobilities' of people, objects, images, information and waste materials have started crossing national borders in a context of continual uprooting and displacement (Urry, 2008; Knowles, 2010). These technical changes have come along with a general ethos of movement and personal development which emphasizes social disjunction and mobility. Boltanski and Chiappello (2009) call this period 'the New Spirit of Capitalism', in which 'The Great' worker must renounce stability to be flexible, mobile, versatile, committed, proactive, and above all: fluid. Others call this moment 'the mobile era' (Urry, 2008) or a liquid/post/late modernity (Urry, 2008; Bauman, 2001; Giddens, 1990). All these studies converge in the sense that we live in a moment marked by detachment, temporariness and accelerated processes of individualization. In other words, we live in a world of increasing mobility: a sphere within which little seems to be permanent, secure, or stable. In December of 2008 I found myself participating in the wonders and sorrows that the "mobile world" has to offer us, since I intended to study English and experience life abroad. Hence, I worked and lived outside of my native Brazil, in London for one year (2008-2009).

On my first day in this huge, concrete metropolis, I remember how amazed I was when I took a bus towards the centre of London and discovered there were Brazilian people speaking Portuguese at my side. I thought I would hear, in the United Kingdom, only the English language. However after meeting so many Brazilians at the English language school where I had enrolled, as well as those in the first house where I lived and seeing so many Brazilian shops spread across important parts of London, such as Oxford Street, I quickly understood how big the "Brazilian community" actually is.

According to the Brazilian Ministry of External Relations (2009) approximately 3.5 million Brazilians are abroad. The main countries of destination are: the United States (1,280,000), Japan (280,000) and European countries such as the United Kingdom (180,000), Portugal (137,000), Spain (125,000), Germany (89,200), Italy (70,000), France (60,000), Switzerland (57,500) and Belgium (42,000). In this context, the UK today is a "target" country for Brazilian migrants. Although the British Census (2011) indicates that there are 50,000 Brazilians living in the UK, analysts and organizations estimate that there are on average 200,000 Brazilians living in the United Kingdom, in London this number varying between 130,000 and 160,000, making this the biggest Brazilian community in Europe (Cwerner, 2002). No wonder then, when I got to London, I felt like I was living in Brazil, but with different weather.

Due to the vast number of Brazilians living in London, the Department of Geography in Queen Mary's University of London conducted research to delineate their socio-economic profile! (Evans *et al*; 2007) According to the data, most Brazilians are young and relatively well-educated, with the majority finishing high school. The survey also shows Brazilians had innumerable reasons to migrate, such as: 25% of the respondents went to London to study and work; 24% to work and save money; 21% were intending to stay in London long-term; 16% wanted to study English; 8% had other interests and 6% did not answer. In relation to occupations, the data indicates that 63% of Brazilian respondents (both male and female) work full-time (thirty-five to forty-eight hours) in jobs considered un-skilled in the service sector such as cleaning, catering, construction, driving and baby-sitting.

Evan *et al*'s study equally shows that the Brazilians researched usually plan to come to London to stay for two or three years before returning to Brazil. Nevertheless, many tended to become undocumented migrants over time after they decided to stay longer than planned, not knowing when they will return. This would be indicative of a constant process of construction and reconstruction of life goals in the trajectories of these migrants. Furthermore, when unpicking the reasons for staying in London, other issues were raised such as consumption, mobility and access to goods and services.

Thus, there are different Brazilians with different reasons to be in London, performing and interacting in the so-called unskilled job sector. It is precisely in these spaces and urban settings, within these migrant bodies, that it is possible to find access points to analyse their trajectories and the skills necessary to have a flexible life in London. It was in such places as these, working as a cleaner, kitchen porter, and waiter that I encountered many different migrant stories.

From my personal experience, therefore, I decided such previously untold stories demanded to be documented as testaments to the courage, as well as the fears, of all those people I met. I quickly realised ethnographic research (Wacquant, 2002) would reveal a great deal about migrant experiences, as it is expressed among Brazilians in London: academic research, on my part, which eventually led to my master's degree. Living with people at the edges of a host society, justified or otherwise, taught me that the very process of noting this human flow often took the form of an encounter with the practicalities of constraint and feelings of "otherness". Indeed, the precarious and unregulated working practices I discovered, along with illegalities in the "Brazilian community", occasionally caused me to ponder about much wider issues.

From listening to their individual stories, I came better to understand the different initial reasons that lead Brazilians to leave their country of origin in order to subject themselves to unskilled work, even when they had a relatively high level of education and qualifications. Those factors helped to define their place of destination, how the processes of displacement and settlement are performed in everyday practices. The importance of friends and family ties (social networks) for integration in the informal/illegal labour market all surfaced as factors adding unforeseen complexities to the unspecified tactics used to stay in London, as well as to projections and personal prospects for their futures.

In the group I observed, no dislocation had been due to forced migration. They were Brazilians belonging to different social contexts in Brazil, with different life-adventures in London, who decided to have a superior life in another country. They were all first generation, living in the country from one to ten years, with different documentary status and forms of "work contract". The vast majority did not have plans for the future seeking to focus their lives in the present, without knowing exactly when they would return to Brazil.

At first, as we will see, when one analyses this group of Brazilians in London, one could try to characterize them as students and workers. However these categories are 'loose' when trajectories are checked. For example, many say they are students but end up just working and not attending school. This same "flexibility" is found when dealing with the issue of legality and illegality. Even those with documentation often cross the barrier of legal and illegal through the social pores that already exist, either by working more hours than is allowed for students, or by performing activities characterized as illegal. We could say that they are all "serving-class migrants" (Knowles and Harper, 2009), working in the service sector. They provide to London the sort of service that they themselves have become accustomed to and, for many, a pertinent reason for staying.

This book is the result of my Master degree's research, along with my personal experience as an migrant in London. It shows the lives, journeys, as well as individual stories, of people on the move in narratives which would otherwise remain invisible, obscure, or unspoken. Yet, before starting our journey through lives which are increasingly mobile, it is important to understand the theoretical and historical context behind Brazilian emigration.

Outlining (Brazilian) Migration

When we analyse studies about contemporary migration flows, the 1980's are seen as the "beginning" of a new "process". Certainly, in the last three decades, migration and "mobilities" have become an important issue in both policy-making and academic agendas. As Urry (2008) affirms, it seems as if the entire world is on the move and there is a sense of "mobility" in the air. Tellingly, Castles and Miller (2009:2) consider this period as "the age of migration" characterised by challenging and emergent social complexities, not to mention changes in spatial reference, where human beings flow, not to mention culturally to circulate, with greater intensity across national borders.

Not through coincidence, emigration became an important issue in Brazil during the same period. Certainly, early studies about this topic considered the economic crisis[1] in the '80s and '90s as a major factor in this movement, which saw Brazilians migrate to industrialised countries looking for better living and working conditions and in some cases to maintain their 'class position' (Margolis, 1994; Sales, 1995; 1999; Goza, 1992; Sasaki, 2000; Torresan, 1994; 2012). In other words, it was a migration of workers belonging to specific segments of the population[2], who felt disappointed with the economic and political situation in Brazil and decided to seek improved opportunities outside. They were "the economic crises expats" who supplied the labour market in the U.S., Western Europe and Japan (Assisi, 2002; Fusco, 2007).

In their host societies, these migrants tend to perform jobs considered to be low-skilled or tasks that the "locals" refuse to do (Ribeiro, 1998;

1 Such restructuring involved the opening of domestic markets to imported products; which in turn resulted in the closure of industrial units, the extinction of secure jobs and an increase in socially informal labour. This had an impact on 60% of the total workforce (Leite, 2009).

2 The majority of the studies mention that Brazilians abroad have a middle class background, without mentioning its meaning. The Strategic Affairs Secretariat of Brazil (SAE) divides the middle class into three sections: the lower middle class, comprising those households with per capita income between R$ 291 and R$ 441, the middle middle class, which is between the income levels of R$ 441 and R$ 641, and finally upper middle class, whose family income is between R$ 641 and R$ 1,019 per capita. At the time of this study £1 was the equivalent of 3,45 Brazilian R$.

Margolis, 1994), such as personal and domestic services (e.g., nannies, maids, cleaners and drivers), which are usually carried out within the informal and sometimes illegal employment sectors. Such occupations are low paid by the standards of local workers and this situation is aggravated by the fact that most migrants do not have legal documentation. This leads to a perception of "lowering" in the occupational status of those workers who define their job as "underemployed" (Ribeiro, 1998). From one angle, these migrants would have exchanged one precarious situation for another. But the alleged gains of working in industrialised countries were conceptualized as being worthwhile due to access regarding higher valued currencies, which would allow them to invest for a possible return.

To some extent, the first studies on Brazilians abroad were wise to follow the globalized perspectives of authors like Sassen (1988) who connect these novel international flows to the powerful economic processes of contemporary globalisation, where the causes of such movements would be linked to a context of disparities in employment, along with incomes and welfare on a planetary scale. In this sense, developing countries would have a tendency to originate migration flows because of the situation of increasing unemployment and lack of prospects for more advantageous conditions of work and life being generated by the process of economic restructuring. This theory would be organized around the model of neoclassical economics "push-pull", which considers "peripheral countries" as a pole of repulsion for workers, while "central countries" act as areas of attraction (Castles and Miller, 2009). As part of the overall economy, international migration would be a redistribution mechanism of workers in different parts of the globe.

The above theoretical view understands migration as the result of a single factor linked to the economy, where the migrant is always the "economic migrant" (Knowles, 2003): the poor who migrate from a region with abundant, although less paid labour, to a developed country with a shortage of labour and wages easily seen as more attractive. Perhaps I need to confess I have always held in my imagination this idea about migrants as poor workers who migrate to a richer place in search of better employment conditions. Yet my experiences as a migrant pointed to something that went beyond the issue of employment and economic desires. Indeed, most of those who migrate and perform informal and low-skilled jobs in the host society do not see economic imperatives as the primary factor. Empirical findings suggest that economic factors are only part of a layer of multileveled reasons in any decision to migrate, thus requiring us to think beyond the "push-pull" theoretical perspective.

According to Knowles (2003), for instance, in the late twentieth century, one out of thirteen people living in the West was an international migrant, many departing from developing countries towards developed ones. Nonetheless, a significant scale of migrants equally leave from developed nations and move to developing ones, such as the 6,000,000 British expats (10% of the population) living abroad. A similar situation is seen in the case of the 500,000 Brazilians, called *braziguayos,* living in Paraguay, which is considered a less developed country than Brazil (MRE, 2009). Unquestionably then, migration should be analysed in a context, not reducing contemporary migrations to the displacement of poor workers towards more developed locations. As Urry (2008) states, being physically mobile has become for both rich and poor a "way of life" across the globe.

In certain circumstances, the greatest propensity for migration doesn't come from the poor but occasionally from the most qualified people, who may inadvertently contribute to the increase of the inequalities between the country of destination and origin (McGovern, 2007). As the following cases show, researches about Brazilian migrants tend to demonstrate the following: they are young, with a middle-class or lower-middle class background in Brazil, along with a relatively high level of education by national standards (Margolis, 1994; Sales, 1999; Assis, 1995; Martes, 1999; Scudeler, 1999; Soares, 1995, Fusco 2007).

Thus previous analysis focusing on exclusively economic issues have been criticized by authors such as Alexander and Knowles (2005), who state that migration studies shouldn't examine the advent of globalization from the economic aspect alone. Clearly, a range of subjective decisions, local facts of life, and historical relations between the societies of emigration and immigration should be taken into account, when researching into the migrating group. Even the notion of necessity/desire takes different forms according to individual lifestyle (Knowles and Harper, 2009). Torresan's pioneering investigations concerning Brazilians in London (1994), for example, showed that some of those interviewed migrated to build a new life experience, far from the dominant patterns of behaviour of Brazilian society.

Studies on Brazilian emigration in the late 90s and 2000s also incorporated a critical approach to the exclusively economic perspective. They started to establish the way in which social network analysis helps in understanding not only the motivations of individual migrants but, in addition, the reasons for choosing their destination in question: how they interact amongst themselves when they arrive in the host country, and how social ties provide facilities and gains during the displacement process (Truzzi, 2008). The success of those who migrated during the "crisis" became the motivation for relatives and friends to follow "in their steps". Put differently, it was no longer the "crisis" in itself that provided the engine behind the decision to migrate but rather the "migrant pioneer" who built a bond with those who stayed in the country of origin (Fleischer, 2002). Due to these factors, there is a creation of migration flows from some Brazilian cities, like Governador Valadares and Criciuma, to some regions of the U.S. (Fusco, 2002; Soares, 2002; Assis, 2003) as well as from other Brazilian regions to some specific countries abroad such as Portugal (Machado, 2005) and Japan (Sasaki, 2000).

These studies focus on the idea of "solidarity networks" which are active among Brazilians who try to help each other in the host society (Soares, 2003; Goza, 2003). However, many of them limit their investigation by only tracing routes and analysing the size of social networks, as well as their importance in the migration project (Assis et al, 2010; Assunção, 2010; Nitahara Souza, 2010), without thinking how these social ties can also work as control and exclusion instruments. What is more, they can make the same mistake that the "economic theorists" did, reducing the reasons to migrate to a single factor, replacing the "*Homo Economicus*" with the "*Homo Solidarius*". For many network authors, the migrant is an actor who relates within his/her community from relationships based on reciprocity and solidarity, without taking into account the conflicts

Willesden Junction High Street, an area in North London has a large number of Brazilian amenities offering the Brazilian community many different kinds of advice and services. These range from English language courses and help with visa issues to Brazilian food stores and clothing outlets.

and competitions existent within the group, which is also exclusionary (Martes and Fazito, 2010).

Framing Brazilian discourses of 'solidarity' abroad

Based on the scenario described above, solidarity within migrant communities is assumed to be central by most researchers, whereas the interest, competition, and conflict within them are largely ignored (Margolis, 2003). Some empirical findings for Brazilians in the US have shown that there is a discourse of 'lack of solidarity' among them which impacts in the formation of their identities abroad (Margolis, 2003; Fusco, 2007). Brazilians in the US frequently complain about a lack of sense of community among fellow countrymen. This situation is further exacerbated by the discourse that Brazilians turn into different people when they are abroad: they do not help each other and only think about making money (Margolis, 2003).

The image of "tenuous solidarity" and the depreciation of Brazilians abroad, arguably impinges on the formation of their identities in this new social context. As a case in point, there is a discourse of "us vs. them" among Brazilians living in New York, Boston and Miami and, in general, it works to create the identity of a superior Brazilian opposed to an inferior one, who is "morally dirty" - rude, ignorant, a redneck. Hence, a context of prejudice and discrimination among countrymen in foreign lands quickly emerges. On the other hand the same process of 'us vs. them' occurs to create a 'Brazilian identity' in opposition to Hispanics or Latinos.

In several places within the U.S, Hispanics act as the "inferior other" to create Brazilian identity from the discourse "we're not like them", since Hispanics are seen as poorer and less educated than the Brazilians. This situation happens in New York (Margolis, 2003), and in Massachusetts (Martes, 2003). Conversely, as stated by Martes (*idem*), no matter how much the Hispanic category is interpreted as exclusive, it cannot mean that Brazilians will not adopt this persona in specific circumstances and in an instrumental way, when they can benefit from the quota system, as happens in Miami where the Hispanic community is well organized politically and so the fact *one* may identify himself/herself as Hispanic may be advantageous.

Oliveira's research (2003) in Miami shows precisely that when migrants seek protection from the prejudice imposed by ethnic classifications and this protection is institutionalized in some places such as in Florida, these subjects link themselves to categories that will bring gains, even though inwardly they say they are not all equal, as is the case of Brazilians who are linked to the Hispanic community in Miami. In other words, in these cases, a Mexican-American, a Dominican, a Puerto Rican and a Brazilian can get together being known as only "Latinos" or "Hispanic", to be able to confront institutionalized racism, build electoral alliances, acquire local power, or gain "space" within an institution. But when they are alone in the company of other Latinos, they discard Latino people and the linking occurs by country of origin.

Curiously, a situation of "management" starts to occur within these ethnic categories and the way they are used is connected to both the local institutional context as well as specific individual situations. Indeed, the local institutional context is as important as the internal characteristics of the group since generational factors, such as the heterogeneity of national groups and social classes, produce internal divisions (Martes, 2003). Consequently, the identity ties of these individuals vary either regarding the institutional environment to which they belong or on a macro level of general identification. Moreover, on micro levels of interaction wherein the immediate situation in which they find themselves is tight, differences are re-established. In New York and Massachusetts the constitution of Brazilian identity contrasts with the inferior figure of the Hispanic, while at the same time those same Brazilians "inwardly" say there is another kind of Brazilian who is not like them (that is, a Brazilian who comes from a low social level, with no training, education, manners and culture is considered less than them as illiterate and poor).

This 'other' inferior Brazilian surfaces in several discourses in the U.S., materializing in the figure of the "*Mineiro*" (people from Minas Gerais), as is the case in Florida since there, those already "established" would tend to be those who live in "Miami-Dade" (who are *Paulistas* – from São Paulo and *Cariocas* – from Rio de Janeiro), while outsiders, like the "*Mineiros*" live in Pompano Beach (Oliveira, 2003). In Miami, there is a local differentiation based on work, which is expressed on the issue of regionalism in Brazil, as in "Miami-Dade" Brazilians are more stabilized and many are traders and businessmen, while in "Pompano Beach" and "Broward", they are performing work deemed unqualified in the service sector, the so-called "migrant labour", and all are called "*Mineiros*".

In London the greatest differentiation occurs among Brazilians themselves. It is common to hear statements that Brazilians migrating to London only think about money and take advantage of their countrymen; they are poor, uneducated and unsupportive. As with the case of New York, this differentiation arises even in a context where the vast majority performs the same kind of precarious work!

From this discussion, we can say that social networks allow us to explain various situations occurring in recent migratory processes. Many of the displacements taking place nowadays are due to the existence of networks, because, as stated by Fusco (2002), the Brazilian migrants (in the same way as others) do not spread randomly around the world but follow in the footsteps of their predecessors, focus on specific destinations and are attracted by the facilities brought by social ties. Nonetheless, one should additionally take into account how these ties are used and the existing conflicts within communities. Such conflicts also reflect on how the identity of these migrants will be built in the receiving country.

It is in this sense that another perspective is gaining strength in migration studies. The idea of lifestyle migration (Knowles and Harper, 2009), which seeks to understand the reasons that prompted emigration and also the complexity of how migrants develop their daily practices and identity in the host society. Such an analytical proposal has no intention of reducing the act of migrating to only a sole factor, nor of excluding the economic issue, but to bring other social variants:

> "Our usage of lifestyle migration is not intended to flatten migration motives to a single dimension. On the contrary, it acknowledges the shifting multiplicity of motives and adds something we consider more important: the operationalization of motives in concrete settlement practices. We think about lifestyle migration as constituted in its settlement practices. Our use of lifestyle migration also acknowledges the inseparability of economic factors like income and the quality of life it supports (Knowles and Harper, 2009, p.11)".

Even though studies on lifestyle migration focus on relatively affluent individuals of all ages, moving to places that are meaningful because, for various reasons, they offer the potential of a better quality of life (Benson and O'Reilly, 2009), I argue that the idea of lifestyle migration should be used not only for "affluent migrants". The (re)negotiation of the work–life balance, the pursuit of a good quality of life and freedom from prior constraints (Benson and O'Reilly, 2009) is not a characteristic of only relatively affluent migrants: these are features present in many different migrant life stories. Thus, the idea of lifestyle migration is important here for not reducing the act of migrating to a single dimension, as well as to take migration as a project which continues long after the initial act of migration.

These last two perspectives (Social Networks and Lifestyle Migration) complement each other and are used in this book to analyse Brazilians in London. For the vast majority of workers interviewed, social networks supplied important information, like the selection of a location for migrating, recommendations of jobs and housing. In other words, the networks acted as an intermediary for the mobility of migrants. However, when analysing trajectories of life, it is noticeable that the diversity of actors with different interests in this group, who perform the same type of work in the receiving society, will influence the way they will relate to others. There are different lifestyles that intersect in the same place, and these migrants build and rebuild these lifestyles constantly.

Researching lives in motion

This book documents the trajectories of different Brazilian migrants, who are performing unqualified labour (cleaners, dish washers and waiters) in London, focusing on their processes of displacement, arrival, adaptation and survival in the host society. It is the result of two different moments in the British capital. The first, nine months (2008-2009) living in the Brazilian community within London, with the aim of studying English and having an experience as an migrant working in the so-called 'unskilled' jobs sector. During this time, I produced a notebook with observations about the work conditions of this group of migrants and their problems faced in the host society. I conducted an ethnography[3], performed as observant participation (Wacquant, 2002) in various types of working environments (cleaner, kitchen porter and waiter) as well as observing Brazilians out of work and looking at their settlement and survival tactics used in the everyday life.

The dense description of various situations of the everyday life of an migrant, presented throughout the text, is the result of this "ethnogra-

3 By ethnography, I use the terms of Wacquant (2002, p. viii), describing it as a methodology in which the researcher performs an "immersion' and even moral and sensual conversion to the cosmos under investigation construed as a technique of observation and analysis that, on the express condition that it be theoretically armed, makes it possible for the sociologist to appropriate in and through practice the cognitive, aesthetic, ethical schemata that those who inhabit that cosmos engage with in their everyday deeds"

phy/participation." It consists of describing the life of an migrant having referenced my own journey as an migrant/worker/researcher.

This "everyday" experience allowed me to access more detailed information, for example, observing the problems and difficulties of being undocumented or the use of drugs at work, situations that I would hardly have accessed if I had only introduced myself as a researcher who wanted to conduct interviews. According to Whyte (2005), referring to his fieldwork, to meet people, get to know them, fit in their activities, he had to spend time with them and by just sitting and listening he got the answers to questions that he wouldn't even have had the idea of asking through interviews. Therefore, that research was the result of interactions in and within the fieldwork. Following Wacquant (2002) in which her associate become a boxer to develop his research, I put myself as "object" and "subject" of observation. The notes came from both a migrant worker in London and a researcher within the field.

The second moment consists of three months in London (2011), in which I conducted in-depth interviews with 17 men and 13 women, trying to analyse the trajectories of a group of Brazilian workers contacted in the previous stay—their lives before leaving Brazil, the process of displacement (arrival and adaptation), the search for work and prospects for the future. The data obtained intersects with my previous experience as a migrant, brought together to create the text.

Six trajectories of life were chosen out of the thirty interviews to write this book. In my view, these stories represented many other cases I have met. I chose six cases that, theoretically, would represent two distinct groups of migrants who are performing unskilled jobs in London. The first group presents the cases of three women who claimed to have migrated to study English but family and gender issues were also important in their decision to migrate. In the second group the trajectories of three men who would fit in the "classic model" of the economic migrant are shown who migrates in order to work, save some money and return to the country of origin. Yet, as will be demonstrated, these categories do not remain pertinent to the migrant after settling in the host society.

The text was constructed as a tour of migrant lives, in which I used my trajectory to structure the reports of migrants. For this reason, sometimes the text will present passages seemingly repetitive because, depending on the situation, the story may repeat itself in the case studies. Therefore, I use the words of Lahire (2004) when introducing his "sociological portraits", that repetition is important information and not a flaw in the writing especially because my intention here is to demonstrate precisely what factors differ in these "migrant experiences".

The first chapter *"The detatchment: arriving and adapting"* describes the process of displacement and arrival of the six cases studied, along with my own experience. This part focuses on the reasons that led these migrants to move and the factors that differentiate their arrival in the 'new' country. Furthermore, the importance of the first house, to get the first job so as to learn the 'codes' of the local society, appears as central to the adaptation process of the migrant. Additionally, adapting varies according to the individual characteristics of each case.

The second chapter, ""*Social networks and work*", besides characterizing the work of cleaner, kitchen porter and waiter, also focuses on the importance of social ties to obtain a first job, as well as to ensure mobility between occupations. On the other hand, it also demonstrates that this mobility varies according to individual attributes and how the same social contacts that mediate these migrants mobility, in many instances, also serve as a tool of "control" and "exclusion" within the work environment.

The third chapter, "*Extending the stay: experiences, consumption, tactics and body*" shows how these migrants start reflecting and reframe their life goals from the moment they start to have some experience in the English capital. At first, there is a hunger for work and many begin to work long hours, even those who had not the initial idea to migrate to work and save up money. In their spare time there is also an enchantment with the lifestyle, marked by parties, consumption and travel, reasons reported to remain in the country longer than planned. Since the idea of the return changes, these migrants are required to use different tactics of permanence and survival. However, over time, that craving for work decreases, because their bodies cannot tolerate much wear and tear, which makes the work rate decrease as the lifestyle changes.

The fourth chapter “”*Community coexistence: status, discrimination and prejudice*”” focuses on the daily lives of these migrants in the way they relate to each other. The first part describes how the idea of migrating is strongly influenced by the culture of “winner”; the individual migrates to win and, therefore, needs to always keep this image of winner, both for those who live in London, and for those who stayed in Brazil. The second part narrates the stories of the picture that Brazilians, who are performing unskilled jobs, have from their countrymen living in the English capital.

The fifth chapter “”*Negotiating the return: freedom, loneliness and permanent present*”, depicts the moment when the idea of “return” begins to be negotiated, as well as the reasons given for settling or not. In this context, loneliness appears as one of the worst problems for many migrants and Brazilian churches emerge as support for some to overcome this feeling. The concluding chapter “*Brazilians in London revisited*” summarizes some analytical findings of the research tying up ideas that were sprayed throughout the text with the descriptions of trajectories of life.

Furthermore, it is important to mention that all names have been replaced by fictitious ones to ensure the safety and privacy of these migrants, many of whom are undocumented migrants. Also, within the book, the use the terms ‘illegal and legal’ will appear to refer to those who have, or do not have, legal documents to stay in the country. I do not use these terms with pejorative undertones, but it should be noted that they are part of the everyday language of a migrant.

Figure 1 – Sociogram

An illustration of the paths I took, as a worker/researcher, which provided, at the same time, access to jobs and housing and to the most different life stories told here. The dashed lines show locations that provided information and knowledge about the possibility of experiencing “such paths”, although I myself have not done so in person. The solid lines show the paths travelled by me as a worker. The following description is based on this illustration.

This picture was taken in one the of interviewees rooms in London.

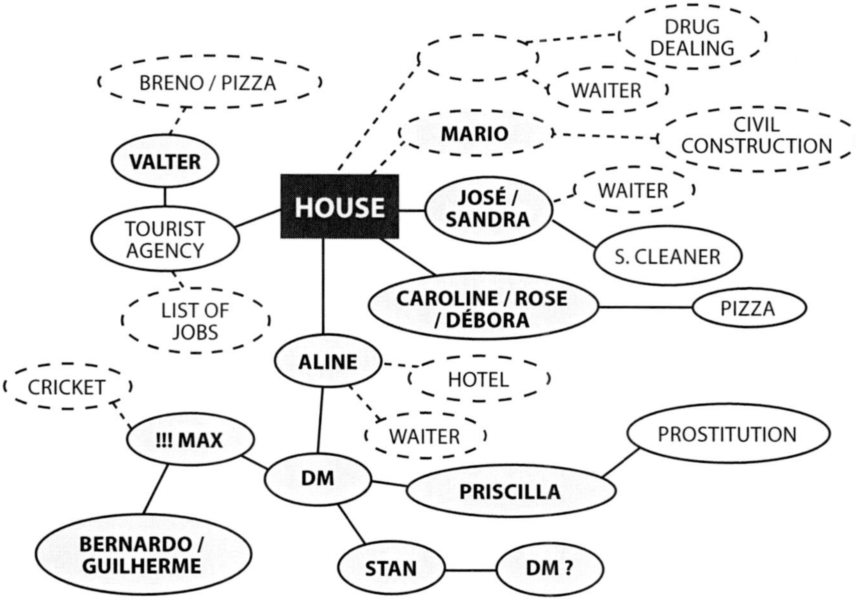

CHAPTER 1

THE DETACHMENT: ARRIVING AND ADAPTING

1.1 Displacement and arrival

The act of migration brings us directly to the issue of spatial mobility. However, this movement requires more than just moving spatially for the migrant; it is necessary for the migrant to disengage, minimally, from himself - built from his place of origin - to be born as an individual into a new society.

As illustrated by SAYAD (1998), emigration is the stage where migrants leave their group and sociocultural space to engage in pursuit of their goals and their arrival is the moment when they are born as an individual into the receiving society, which has practically no knowledge of everything that precedes the moment of this birth. The arrival is the end of one journey and the beginning of a new one; a new life in a new location (KNOWLES and HARPER, 2009). Yet, the way this happens varies with the characteristics of each individual's trajectory.

This birth into the receiving society occurs in the Immigration Control, which can be a smooth and simple experience for some and traumatic for others. The "traumatic birth" happens to those who do not have European documentation and would fit into stereotypes of possible "illegal" migrants: young people from poorer countries who do not have ties in the country of origin which would prove their return (labour, assets, etc.), and do not have much money to stay in the receiving country.

In my case, I was the youngest son of a retired fire fighter and a manicurist and who grew up in a small town in the state of São Paulo. Although my family was economically considered as "lower class", I had access to certain goods and services in the city due to the social ties that my parents had, which facilitated my association with people regarded as belonging to the "upper middle class", sharing some "signs of that group", if one may say so.

Through social contacts that my mother established with her customers, added to the fact that I had always been considered as a good student, I was able to attend the last years of high school with scholarships at private schools, though I studied up to the seventh grade in public schools. In this case, it was through my mother's network that I had access to private education. Nonetheless, it probably would not happen if I did not have the necessary attributes to be a scholarship student; they never let me forget that I had to be a good student for the school and the "reliable friend"- the scholar who did not smoke and did not drink – either for the owners of the school or the parents of my friends.

During my time in high school I always wanted to travel to another country on one of these student exchange programs, as some of my schoolmates had done. My family, however, was unable to afford the costs. Therefore, when I was in my sophomore year at university I got a research initiation scholarship and I saved all the money in order to live an experience in another country4. This idea came up when I met

4 Just prior to going to University my father and my brothers opened a small business in the field of transport. This new family business provided a more favorable financial position, allowing me to live and study in another city.

a friend, Valter, who was going to London to spend time there with his brother Breno, who had been living in England for two years. Valter gave me all the information required to migrate, as well as the agency he used and a possible work contact at a pizzeria where his brother worked. Hence, in December 2008, I embarked towards Europe with Diego, a friend who I shared student lodgings with and who also wanted to have some life experience in England and learn English.

When I arrived at immigration in London there were two queues of people passing through: one for people connected to the European Union and another for people connected to the rest of the world. Diego did not speak any English. I teased him in the line: "You are white, Italian-faced, look at that nose! You probably will not have many problems." Coincidence or not, that's exactly what happened. The immigration officer asked if Diego spoke English, he answered no and gave the papers and passport to the agent who analysed them for about five minutes and stamped it.

When it was my turn, they asked the same question about the language, I said I spoke a little. Then they began to question me about what I was doing there, the reason why I wanted to learn English, what my father's profession was, if he was rich, among other questions that took more than forty minutes. When I had shown all the papers that the travel agency had sent me and had tried to answer all questions, even considering that I was feeling very nervous and could no longer understand any of them, the agent looked at me and said he would let me pass.

It was a tense moment, and for the first time in my life I felt what it was like to be in a situation of outright discrimination. The whole network of people, capital and attributes (whether material or symbolic) that have always been behind me, started to seem worthless: I was an migrant begging permission to enter a country.

The experience at Immigration Control was a rite of passage, a symbolic kind of torture that generated a feeling of being controlled at all times. As stated by Clastres (1990) "an initiated man is a marked man," with the goal of initiation being, in its moment of torture, the body marking, since with the initiatory ritual that society prints its mark on the body of the young. Torture is not just a personal endurance test, whose success guarantees social approval, but the injury left by it establishing a social belonging; it is a pedagogy that goes from the group to the individual. Consequently, the experience left its mark on me, and with other people that I interacted with in England also left, the brand of control. Whenever I had to go through immigration I was nervous, as if I was doing something forbidden and would be discovered at any time. Even my English, that had much improved, I used to forget.

This frustrating passage through Immigration Control appears in several paths, as well as in the path of the cousins Bernardo and Guilherme, who had to be a little more 'flexible' to get into the country.

1.1.1 Bernardo and Guilherme

Bernardo and Guilherme grew up in Araçatuba, a small town in the state of São Paulo. Coming from low income families, they didn't complete high school; they would fit the typical style of migrants present in our imagination, the "economic migrant"; one who migrates from a poorer region in search of work and better financial conditions elsewhere. In the 1990s there was a "fever" of people from Araçatuba that migrated out of the country and always came back with money, a fact that made many of the youth of this town have the dream of leaving Brazil, working for a time in the U.S. or Europe, accumulating all their earned money and then returning to start their own business.

> It was very common to hear about someone that went to Portugal, you always heard about Japan, the U.S. also, so I had to leave. They returned, buying a car, buying land, paraded, and I came from a very poor family, so I saw it as an opportunity for me [Guilherme].

Bernardo, the older cousin, was the first to migrate. In 2004, aged twenty-six, he worked in a factory of engines of small wash tubs and cabinets in his town. Earning R$ 560.00 per month, he used to say that he had no future in that company. Because he had a neighbour living in the U.S., he first tried to get a visa for that country, which was denied. After spending a lot of money on it, Bernardo stayed home and he became unemployed for two months. During this period, he used some of the money from his settlement with the firm where he worked and financed a bike. In addition, he also bought a car and despite it being "the consumerist madness" of someone who was unemployed, it was precisely because of the car that Bernardo went to London.

> There were three brothers who lived here (London) thirteen years ago; called the Palermo brothers. They would often go to Brazil, to my city, buying big cars to joy ride. One time when they were in Brazil they ended up spending all their money, and had to sell some cars. When they were returning to London, I bought one of their cars from them. I only gave them half the money they needed at the time, and said that I would pay the balance gradually. In this context of owing them money we became friends. I sent a little bit and then I sent another little bit and asked him: "Brother, and how is life there (London)?" He said, "Ah, there is jobs here for everyone". I decided to move to London and they said they were going to help me, especially because I owed them money and if I was there on their side working, then they knew I would pay them back the money that I owed [Bernardo].

After the contact with the Palermo brothers, Bernard sold his motorbike and the car and with the money he bought a ticket to London. He boarded the plane as a tourist and was going to try for a student visa when he arrived at the airport. As he did not speak English and had nothing to prove that he had ties that would make him return to Brazil, he was held back at the Immigration Control and taken to an interrogation room.

> They called again (for the fifth time). The woman looked at me and asked again: "What are you doing here?" with a translator. I said, "Ah, I came here to study. "Studying what?" "I'm learning English". "Which school are you going to?" I said: "The Metropolitan College." They asked if all I had said was true, because if it was a lie I would be judged in the court of that country. After a lot of questioning, they asked I had something to say, I said: "Oh, yes I have actually, I did not know that I would be so unwelcome in a first world country." The woman asked the translator: "What did

> he say?" He then translated it. She said to him: "Tell him that he isn't the first or the last and tell him to shut up." I went crazy. I got up and asked, "Where is my suitcase? Where's my money? I want to leave now. I do not need this here." I stood up and said, "Nice to meet you, nice to meet you" and in Portuguese, 'fuck you". They stood face to face with me... The guy sent me back to the room... After ten minutes he came and said: "Look, it was a pleasure to meet you, like you said, but you were deported; grab your suitcase and follow me." I followed, right, man?! But then we arrived at the roulette there and he turned to me and said: "Welcome to the United Kingdom!" The guy was joking; they had let me enter the country [Bernardo].

Three years later, in 2007, his cousin Guilherme, aged 25, followed in Bernardo's footsteps and ended up going through a similar type of embarrassment. At the time Guilherme was working at a petrol station in the state of Mato Grosso do Sul, when he decided to try life in Spain with a friend from work.

> My friend managed to talk to the guy there (in Spain) and the guy told us to go to Seville, that he would help us in the beginning. I resigned from the petrol station, I made the settlement, I financed the ticket, I sold the motorbike I had, and the money raised was enough to buy a ticket and keep some money in reserve for the beginning [Guilherme].

When he was ready to leave, his friend discovered that his father had cancer and for that reason he would not go to Spain anymore. Guilherme said he would not miss that opportunity because, as he himself says, it was his hour. So he just asked his friend to check with the contact in Spain if everything was all right and he still would go.

> I went, however, and the guy didn't wait for me in Madrid, would you believe it? I stayed four days in Madrid without knowing anything. I had saved a few euros from the settlement and I was sleeping in a hostel. I had about two thousand euros, so I didn't go hungry or any other kind of need, but I was alone, desperate, and despite not knowing the language, Spanish was easy to un-

> derstand and get by. Then I remembered my cousin in London, I had picked up his phone number with my aunt. I called him from Spain, and he said: "Come to London I'll help you, but come through Scotland that is smoother." [Guilherme].

That's exactly what Guilherme did, however, and he ended up having trouble at Immigration in Edinburgh.

> I thought it would be easy because in Spain the guy asked me, "What are you doing here?" I said: "I came for tourism; the company I work for in Brazil gave me the ticket and ten days here in Europe." I argued that I was a car salesman and that year I was the one who sold more cars. I invented this story. I knew I had to invent something good. The guy asked if I had booked into a hotel, I had booked into two hotels. I informed the reserves and entered the country without any problems. In Scotland this excuse didn't work [Guilherme].

In Scotland they did not believe that Brazilian companies were giving that kind of prize to workers. After hours of interrogation, they held Guilherme's passport and a significant part of his money; he was asked to return to the airport the next day, since he had to return to Spain and there was no flight anymore that day. Getting by with the little money he had and the English learned from TV, Guilherme managed to spend the night in a hotel and go to London by train the next day, leaving behind his passport.

After hearing the whole story and the problems he faced to get to London, many would say that he was brave, and he was told on the day of the interview:

> Brave, no! It was really desperation. I came from a very poor family, it was the chance to change my life; it was what I had for myself. It was the only shot I had. I remember when I first came here in 2008 and people were talking about crisis in the U.S., crisis in Europe. When they asked me, I would say: crisis?! Crisis I lived in Brazil for 26 years, there is no crisis here; crisis was my life before [Guilherme].

After this experience, Guilherme says that he stayed almost one year leaving home to work and nothing else, because the experience at immigration made him feel like he was being followed by a policeman all the time.

Today I lost that fear (to go out on the streets). I usually don't like going out much, and I was scared to death... Any police officer that I saw on the street I thought he was from the Immigration coming to get me [Guilherme].

1.1.2 Rose

Despite having different reasons for migrating, and belonging to a different background, Rose, who also spoke no English, had a traumatic arrival. Born in Bolivia and raised in the city of Rio de Janeiro, her father worked in the Bolivian embassy in Rio and her mother was a housewife. The fourth of six children (four men and two women) she had always been considered the "black sheep of the family", the one who liked to drink, go out to parties and did not want to study much.

Despite having grown up in a family with good financial conditions, Rose considers her family as problematic: she always had relationship problems with her parents, especially with her mother, who by being submissive to a sexist family, reproduced the same type of dominance with respect to how to raise her children, teaching women to be submissive to men (FREYRE, 2003).

> My mother always defended men too much, and my father, of course, with the girls, it's just that we always lost, because they were... To my mother, a man can do everything and woman can do nothing. Always complaining that I cannot sew, I cannot cook, I don't know how to wash the dishes, I don't know shit! [Rose].

Rose finished high school and started in the school of business administration, but she didn't like it and ended up dropping out of school in the first year. As she wasn't in college and couldn't stand the control exercised by her mother, she began looking for a job, because she believed that if she acquired financial independence she could do whatever she wanted. With a recommendation from one of her sisters-in-law, she started working as a saleswoman in a famous designer store. Because she wanted so much to work in this place,= and because she got this job through the recommendation of her brother's wife, she worked hard and never said no to the managers, as she felt obliged to work whenever she was requested to. As a result, she became valued by the manager and soon began to rise within the company.

> That's when I started to beat sales quotas… My name began to appear at the top, among the first of the entire network... I was selling a lot, earning well, and as store managers all know each other, there was always someone phoning me and asking me to work for them. So I've always worked in every store I wanted, except "Osklen" and I really wanted to work at Osklen, but I needed to speak English to work there and I knew nothing of English [Rose].

This could lead one to believe that Rose's departure to the city of London would be linked to the fact that she wanted to learn English, in order to get a job at the store that she so desired, However, the family issue was the reason that weighed most in her decision to migrate.

> I never said it was because of English and it is not also to save money... Why I came to London? My younger brother decided to come to London, I don't know why, with his girlfriend. Then he dragged over my other brother. I was right there, I was the assistant manager at "Merizaide" when I decided to come to London, but my younger brothers went to London. My sister turned eighteen and ran away, she said she couldn't stand my parents anymore; she ran away and got married. She went to live in Uruguay with a Uruguayan. Another brother lives in the U.S. and another was married in Rio. Then I noticed: "I'm going to live with my mother alone!!" So I decided to come here when I saw that I really was going to stay with my mother alone. It wasn't because I don't get along with my mother. My mother is a lovely person, a great mother, but as a mother of men. I fight with her all the time. We have always had loud arguments [Rose].

In an attempt finally to escape her mother's control, she called her older brother, who is an engineer in Rio, and under the pretext of studying English and the longing for her younger brothers she asked him to pay her ticket to London and an English course. Rose quit her job as an assistant manager and left, at the age of 32, in 2008.

Rose didn't leave Brazil with a student visa and she meant to apply for one when she arrived at the country. However, that year migration rules had been changed and she could no longer apply for a student visa when she arrived in the UK; this should have been done while she was still in Brazil. She didn't speak any English and a translator was called who explained the situation. Rose was upset with what happened, but as she understood it was just a matter of changes to the law, she had not perceived herself as an "illegal" migrant. The situation changed a bit when she was taken to the place where deported people waited for their flights; it was then that she really felt what the word "migrant" meant in that context.

> Dude, I felt very humiliated, they asked thousands of questions, I had to take off all my clothes, and my fingerprints were taken, even "fingerprints" from my clitoris were taken; there were so many fingerprints. The cell was the type you see in movies, two-storey cement bed, TV attached to cement, there was nothing, the bathroom was a hole, the sink was a button one. The window was protected too. The only thing I had was a white plastic chair, I said: "If I stay here one more day, I'll break that chair and cut myself, but I'm not staying one more day here". And those doors, that had those holes that they opened and passed the food underneath. Dude, wow, I felt very bad, very bad, I couldn't sleep at all. There was no heater because it was fucking cold, but there was a quilt, I was disgusted... I never set foot in a prison, I never did anything. In a prison?! The next day, at three o'clock they were taking us to the airport... when you arrived at the airport your suitcases have a lot of papers saying deported, deported, deported, I died of shame, I died. It's a way of humiliating people! [Rose].

She returned to Brazil, hid from friends because of the shame that she had experienced and decided to return to London. If people saw her in

Rio, she would have to explain what happened and say that she had been arrested and deported, a fact she would never admit to. After performing all necessary procedures to obtain the visa, she returned to London and this time had no trouble entering. However, the symbolic mark of that occurrence remained. She was afraid of everything, did not speak with anyone; became afraid to walk the streets and in the subway. She always had that feeling of being watched by someone and that anything could happen at any time.

In contrast, those who left Brazil with student visas and all necessary documentation to enter the country did not experience the same embarrassments, as in the case of Aline and Priscila who had, besides the student visa, money, proof of accommodation and a letter from a school.

1.1.3 Aline

Aline's story resembles that of Rose in the sense that she migrated in order to "escape" from some family issues and experience the feeling of being an individual living alone in a metropolis. Unlike Rose, Aline was considered as the head of the family and always felt very pressured by it. Born and raised in Rio de Janeiro, the middle child among four siblings (one man and three women), she grew up in a religious middle class family, which made her circle of friends always restricted to that environment. However, as she grew older, she wanted new experiences and she began to conflict with what she felt and with things that church people and her parents said about what is right and what is wrong.

> We (she and her siblings) had this upbringing; my father was always very strict with us. We didn't have much contact with the world, in our childhood, in our adolescence... And then we went to the Baptist Church, then our friends there were the church people. The mates we went with to the mall, to the movies, to the beach, were always the same mates. Then, you grow up in another cycle... Except that when I was seventeen I started dating. My boyfriend was also from the church, and you start to hear those things, that you're wrong and such, and you start to feel bad. Then I got out (of the church). He (boyfriend) got out first, afterward I got out too. I never went back. Because that is the age when you

> start going out, when you start drinking... You start to have sex with your boyfriend and such [Aline].

Aline continued with her first boyfriend for about five years. Things were fine financially, since he was the manager of a famous designer store for women at a mall in Barra da Tijuca and had finished his schooling at the school of tourism. She had always wished to leave Brazil, but as she intended to get married soon she didn't think about the possibility. However, her life changed with the end of her relationship.

> In fact, London is a consequence of several complicated things that happened. My boyfriend, who I dated for about five years, broke up with me, and then it was difficult for me to recover from that. I was in a bad shape. I went through two years of therapy. I could not accept it because for me he was the perfect man for my life... And I had problems at my house; all the time most of the problems were left over for me, everything on me. And I remember in therapy that my doctor said that I had no son, I had no grown-up son, I couldn't try to solve the problems of my father, my mother and my brothers. I tried to start assimilating it. I said no, it really won't do [Aline].

That was when, at twenty-nine years of age, in 2006, she decided to leave and get away from all these problems. She gave notice at work, observing the period of notice and decided to migrate to any country. She thought first of Australia; however, she opted for England, London, due to the facility to visit other European countries. She researched the internet and paid for an English course, she found a house to live in and got a student visa. With the money she received from the sale of her car, and some more she had saved, she went to London with the intention of isolating herself for a while.

> I had this mentality that I was going to live alone in my corner... I was going to work with anything, but I was going to live my life, and my head would be in peace. I didn't know anyone who lived in London or anything [Aline].

Thus, Aline did not migrate following the footsteps of those who had already moved, she had no structured support for when she arrived in

London. As in my case, the only thing she had as certain was the place she was going to stay and her English course. As there was no work in view, information about work and how an migrant should lead a life, she would only learn from the ties she was still going to create on her arrival.

1.1.4 Priscila

Like Rose and Aline, Priscila didn't have as a major factor for her displacement the need for work or because she wanted to learn English, even though her visa was a student one and the excuse given to everyone was always the issue of language. Actually, Priscila wanted, just as the previous two, to "escape" the control exercised by the family, more specifically, in her case, the control of her mother and grandmother. She sought to live for the first time away from the model of life that her grandmother had imposed on her mother and was trying to impose on her. Despite always feeling this pressure, as happened with Aline, it was the end of a long courtship that encouraged this attempt to "become free" in another country.

> My grandmother married my grandfather, who was a doctor, and she also wanted to be a doctor, but she never studied because her father, who was also a doctor, took her from college when mixed classes started in school because an honest girl didn't study in college with men. Then she grew up with this narrow mind, dominating everyone, because the family is large. Everyone has to be just like her and she raised the whole family inside that little world. Then everyone lived in there and lives to this day and I hate that. And my mother married my father, who is completely different from her, because my father does not live like that, and that's why the marriage ended. I'm a lot like my father because I don't live like that either; I hate it to this day. And they want to fit you in. You had to shape yourself to the way they are, you need to be a virgin before getting married, bring your boyfriend to your house for lunch on Sundays. I never took my boyfriend there, ever. To give you an idea, my aunt menstruated and she didn't know what it was, you know! My family is like that, everyone fits into my grandmother's way. I am the only grandchild who does not fit into her way. So I didn't get along with my mother, because deep inside my mother wants to do what my grandmother wants because everyone does and she is her mother [Priscila].

At twenty-seven years of age she had graduated in Business Administration and was working in the finance department of Coca-Cola in Recife. She was well economically, with a steady job in a big company, but could not stand more discussions with her mother and ending the relationship with her boyfriend made her start looking for some way to be free and out of all the pressure.

As Priscila knew some women who lived in London, she contacted them to inquire about the procedures for travelling, for getting a visa, etc. In September 2006, she travelled to London with a friend from work, on a student visa.

1.1.5 Max

Max was another whose arrival had no major problems at immigration. The fourth son, five in total, from a family of Portuguese descent that migrated to São Paulo in the mid-twentieth century, he was born and raised in Capão Redondo, a suburb of the city of São Paulo known to be very violent. His family had always been the owner of businesses in the neighbourhood. They had a Car Wash and a Forwarding Agent business.

Being the son of an migrant mother, he used to say he always wanted to travel and see the USA and Portugal, but had never had the opportunity until now. That was when, in 2002, he began planning a life outside of Brazil for a year to learn English. At that time he worked at Varig Airlines, in Congonhas airport. He held the position of operations manager and had a good salary. As his girlfriend also worked at the same company, and both aimed to grow within it, they decided they needed to move out for a while to improve their English and return to Brazil with a foreign qualification, which would help them to climb within the company.

> We wanted to leave the country in order to study English. We wanted to go to California, but there was that terrorist attack business in the U.S. and it became even more complicated to get the visa, and besides that, we didn't know anyone in California [Max]

Picture taken in one of the interviewees bathrooms. This is the style of bathroom which "shocks" many Brazilian newcomers who are not familiar with the local architecture.

Because the parents of his girlfriend were very conservative Max had to marry her, in order for them to travel together. Already married, they decided to travel to London because they knew some people from their neighbourhood who lived there. As with Bernardo and Guilherme in their city, history repeated itself in Max's neighbourhood: in the 1990s, someone from this small town, or neighbourhood, immigrated to London and returned to Brazil flaunting money and a happy life. And after that, many people started to want the same lifestyle, following in the footsteps of those who had left before, constituting a flow of people towards London. Yet, in the case of Max, he just told his friend he was going to London, saying that if help was needed, he would get in touch.

As he didn't want a close association with the people from Capão Redondo, in London he paid for an English course and rented a house for a month, through an agency, carrying out the entire process by himself. He didn't have his Portuguese documentation yet (which he would provide a year later), thus he would be leaving for England with a tourist visa. After giving notice at work and saving money for almost a year, Max, twenty-nine years old at the time, immigrated for the first time[5] with his wife to London in April 2003. His original intention was to learn English and go back after a year when their visas expired.

He was an employee of Varig in Brazil and he wore the badge of the Company to enter England, since his friends from work had told him to take the badge and say that he was travelling on vacation, and because Varig Company was well known, he would have no problem at Immigration. To enter England, therefore, was quite smooth; the problem came afterwards with the adaptation.

1.2. The house and the adaptation

The first house of a migrant is always important for his adjustment process in the new space. Most of the time the Brazilians in London have as their first house a Brazilian home, since it functions as the place where Brazilian cultural practices and social norms are prevalent – such as Christmas parties, New Year's Eve, barbecues, birthdays, etc.[6] – that is, it is in this house where attempts are made to reproduce national identity and inherited val-

5 Following his return to Brazil after a year, Max got his Portuguese citizenship and returned to London with his wife to work, earn money and build a house in Brazil. Realizing that it was easy to earn money there, and impressed with the ease of consumption, Max didn't want to return to Brazil, not even when he finished building his house. As his wife was very attached to the family, they ended up leaving London for the second time, but they couldn't stand, however, the control of his wife's parents over their relationship. He returned to London after six months in Brazil, for the third time, but now single and alone.

6 This made me think about the Christmas I spent at home with these residents, since the celebration of this date has always been something that I never gave much importance to in Brazil, but when I was in London I made a point of attending the dinner with them and then continue celebrating Christmas drinking and talking, instead of going to night spots, as I always did in Brazil. I remember being upset because everyone participated in the secret Christmas gift exchanges game and I could not take part of it because when I arrived in London the drawing of names had already taken place. It was as if I tried to reproduce a "Brazilian life" outside Brazil, which somehow gave me a sense of belonging and connected me with my life in Brazil, even though I've never played, or indeed given much importance to this lifestyle in my country.

ues. Moreover, the house is also the place where the Brazilian migrant meets other Brazilian residents after a day's work, to talk and to recount the anxieties and difficulties encountered in everyday life (DIAS, 2010).

Another importance of the house is that for these Brazilian workers, the first work almost always comes from the bonds that are created in this place. History repeats itself here, such as when Durham (1984) analysed the cases of domestic migration and shows that it is always among the groups of primary relationships that the migrant obtains and sorts out information about job opportunities. This "primary relationships" group acts as a mediator between individuals and society, being the single supporting point from which migrants have to start the process of adjustment to their new life. Furthermore, in many cases, the migrant's career is conditioned by the occupational experience of the primary relationships group in which he participates.

In many cases, the first house is the starting point to adapt both to the values and codes of local conduct, and to the language, climate and work.

The first house I lived in was owned by a Brazilian couple who had lived in London for some time. The couple had a "real estate company" that worked in conjunction with travel agencies in Brazil. The travel agencies in Brazil would provide regular tenants for the couple and in exchange they would give the tenants paperwork to prove they had already paid for residence in the UK which was needed as proof when passing through Immigration Control. Besides the houses, inside the "real estate company" they also performed "financial transactions" with Brazil. It was the place through which Brazilians in London sent their money to their relatives' bank accounts.[7]

This property portrays well the households where migrant workers live. A small house, where the kitchen, living room and "laundry" - as the washing machine is almost always in the kitchen due to lack of space – are separated by just a counter, with two bedrooms on the bottom

7 This couple's case coincides with the cases analysed by Dias (2010), when demonstrating that in London there is a large Brazilian trade on the rental of houses, where many landlords are stabilized migrants in the country who rent their houses to their countrymen as a profitable way to live.

and three upstairs. There are two small bathrooms where people bathe standing in a bathtub that has a hand shower hanging on the wall[8].

The houses, in their vast majority, are old and have great problems, such as rats in almost all homes and the terrible bed bugs that haunt the sleep of residents. In 2008, the rent was paid weekly, and the price varied according to the area[9] where the house was located and to how many people shared the bedroom. In a house in zone 1 or 2, with one or two people sharing the bedroom, the prices ranged between £65.00 and £85.00 stirling per week, with taxes included. The price of a week of integrated transport - bus and subway for seven days - between zones 1 and 2 was £24.20 stirling, for zone 3 this value rose to £28.40, but the workers who lived there reloaded the value on their cards to use the bus only, since the rate dropped to £13.00. Much time was lost, however, because bus trips in London are time-consuming.

In my case, for example, when speaking of residents, there was only one Italian sharing a bedroom with me; the others were Brazilian. My roommate's name was Ivan, he was twenty-three years old and belonged to a middle class family in Italy. He went to live in England in order to learn English and experience new things. At the beginning he found work in an Italian pizzeria, since he didn't speak English. His first job, as in most cases of migration, was in a place where there were people of his community (RIBEIRO 1998; GOZA 2003)[10]. This not only facilitates the access to information about work, but also communication.

8 Much as the description of the bathroom can be an ethnocentric vision, modeled on the "standard" of Brazilian bathrooms, it is important to highlight how this style of bathroom "shocks" many Brazilians newcomers who are not familiar with the local architecture. In a talk about the different things that have marked these migrants when they arrived in London, the model of "shower" in the bathtub is something that always comes up in the comments. And the most interesting is that, over time, people become used to the aesthetics of the place, with smells and tastes that once were not part of their world and that now mark their beginning in a new society. Gradually, it also becomes their world, so that odd smell, sight or taste, characteristic of the place, is no longer strange or even noticeable (KNOWLES, 2003).

9 The City of London is divided into 6 zones for the purpose of calculations of tariffs on public transportation. These zones are concentric circles with the most central being Zone 1 in the middle. When using public transportation, the more zones you cross, the more expensive is the trip. This must be taken into account when choosing a neighborhood to live. But on the other hand, the neighborhoods nearest the centre are always more expensive. Source: <http://www.yeslondres.com/exibirartigo.asp?articleid=1>.

10 Ribeiro (1998) demonstrates how ethnic or national stereotypes can potentially be elements of friction and conflict while they are markers that define ethnic niches in the

As time went by, Ivan realized that he wasn't learning English or gaining the new experiences that he originally wanted, since he practically lived in a "mini Italy" within London and besides, the Italians exploited him. It was then that he moved to a house with Brazilians and got a job as a waiter in an English events agency. With the improvement of his English, and by increasing his social networks - mainly Brazilians - Ivan got tired of working as a waiter and began trafficking synthetic drugs used by young people in the nightspots because, as he said, "They yielded more money and he spent every day in some different party." Ivan had the ease of getting into this new activity due to the contact that he started having with a bunch of Brazilian people who sold drugs at parties.

Speaking of Brazilians living in the house, there was Mario, thirty-five years old. He had lived in England for seven years and worked in construction but still didn't speak English. Aline and Caroline, both thirty-two years old, had been there more than two years, spoke English and had the best jobs. Aline was a waitress "team leader" at an 'events company' while Caroline was a waitress in a network of pizzerias and was training to become an assistant manager. The rest of the staff worked as cleaners, José (nineteen years old) and Sandra (twenty-seven years old) cleaned stadiums for S. Cleaner[11] and sometimes worked as a waiter and waitress for a Brazilian agency, while Rose and Deborah (both twenty-nine years old) worked as cleaners in the same pizzeria as Caroline. Almost everyone there had worked at S. Cleaner, and it was always someone at the house who got a job for the others.

Going back to my own case, on the first day I already felt the "community spirit" present in the house, even though I didn't share it. At night I realized that, as people kept coming, everyone headed to the living room to talk about how the day had been for each of them. They said, for example, how the work was busy or that the manager had yelled at someone, or even that they had worked many hours that day and on the weekend they

labour market. Goza (2003) in his study of Brazilian workers in Canada noticed that cultural and linguistic ties were what gave employment to a significant number of Brazilians employed by both Brazilians and Portuguese. However, many of them felt exploited by their own countrymen.

11 Company responsible for cleaning show places and events, as well as commercial buildings.

would have "done" a high number of work hours. In this case, the house, as stated by Da Matta (1997), would be a metaphor of Brazilian society, where there are no individuals and all are people. It is a special area, in contrast to the street which follows the logic of impersonality. The house is defined as the space of "love", "caring" and human warmth, while the street would be the reverse, an area defined as a dangerous place belonging to the "government" or the other "people", where new habits and codes of conduct need to be assimilated and incorporated as soon as possible so that the migrant can get around the city (DIAS, 2010).

The adaptation process and also the arrival vary with the characteristics of each trajectory. When one analyses the history of those who came to London without speaking English, for example, it is notorious how the street becomes this dangerous unknown space and how the mobility of these migrants is limited when compared to those who already spoke English, even minimally, when they left Brazil.

From Day One, my friend Diego started to recognize the street as a dangerous space. Before reaching home we passed a fast food restaurant to eat something. Due to my English being a little better than his by then, it was always me who was trying to interact with people on the street to ask for directions. Ordering food, admittedly, should have been an easy thing theoretically, so I told Diego to try and I explained that he could just say "Can I have" and the number of the snack he wanted. Diego's attempt wasn't very successful, because when the girl asked what he would like to drink (this was outside the interaction rehearsed script), he became unresponsive and had to call me to complete the order. Thereafter, Diego avoided going out alone as much as possible, spending hours inside the room and said that if he could work with the rest of the household - who worked doing housekeeping with a group of Brazilians – it would be enough, since he no longer wanted to strive to understand people.

Max was another who felt the language issue as one of the worst factors in his adaptation. As his first home didn't belong to Brazilians, the house itself was seen as a "dangerous" location.

> There were people there from various countries (student house), and we had paid only three weeks for the house, after that we had

> to struggle to continue paying for the house. But in the beginning it was very hard, my girlfriend spoke English but I didn't. I spoke nothing. I was too ashamed to go out, talk to people and such [Max].

The fact of being in a completely unknown city, with no knowledge of the language and not having any known person to help, since he didn't want to live with the folks from Capão Redondo, made Max feel very frustrated in the beginning. He felt bad for not being able to communicate with people; he hardly left the house preferring to stay at home studying and he didn't miss classes.

> I wanted to learn English, I was neurotic. I was concerned for not speaking and for not understanding what people were saying to me. I felt very bad. I kept watching Teletubbies when I was at home because they repeated the words and I repeated together with them. They said "good morning", I said "good morning". "This is a chair" and pointed to the chair, and I would say: "This is a chair". Once I went to buy a phone card, I said the wrong name of the card and the guy gave me this card and said something I didn't understand. I took the card and left saying "Thank you" and smiling at the guy, and I didn't even know what the guy was talking about! We left the convenience store with the card and my wife said: "Do you know what he told you?" I said: "Oh, I don't know, I just know that I said 'Thank you', he gave me the card and I left." "He told you not to hang his language because you are offending him." This guy was an Arab and was saying that I was hanging his language; the bastard is not even an Englishman! I wanted to go back there to fight with the guy and she said: "Why do you want to fight, you cannot even argue with him." I was even more pissed off because I couldn't even defend myself in this country [Max].

As a result of not speaking English, his life was restricted in London to that space he had as a family, along with the 189 bus route which made the journey from his home to the school.

> On our second day the mistress of the house just said to my wife: "Oh, go on the street there, take the 189 bus and get off at the final

> stop and you will see the school there." We had no idea where to go; I had no notion of what the final stop was, I knew nothing. Everywhere I went I was already thinking: "Man, now I don't speak English, I'm *fucking* away from home, and if I get lost I'm *screwed*, I don't go back to Capão Redondo ever again!" [Max].

As much as the question of language, in my case, was not as problematic as I had a basic knowledge of English and I could get by, I also suffered in the first months with the process of adaptation to the new location, both to learn my way around the city in the first weeks and to get a job. Although I had gone to live in a house full of Brazilians, I had first to gain their trust in order to get help.

The person actually ended up helping us in the process of adaptation to the city was José. He took us walking in the neighbourhood where we lived and showed us the buses and subways we should use, in addition to taking us to a store to buy the Skype Phone.[12]

Among the various things that José showed to us over the first few weeks, one very important act was to teach us how to walk in the supermarket and find the cheap products. As he used to say, "Let's go to the supermarket and I'll teach you how to be poor in London." José was referring to the "reduced area"– a part of the supermarket where the products had discounts for having validity periods near the expiry date. Especially in the beginning, saving is very important and the most practical way to do this is to eat less and consume the cheapest products available. José, therefore, was the one who originally taught us to be an migrant in London and who later on got us a job and gave us more confidence to "face" the city.

Rose, Bernardo, Guilherme and Priscila didn't have many adaptation problems initially, because although they didn't speak English, they went to live with people they knew in their first homes. This facilitated their learning how to move around the city as well as in getting a first job.

---

12 Cheap mobile phone, widely used by Brazilians due to having the Skype program that allows people to use it to communicate, thus not having to pay for the phone call.

In contrast, Aline went to live with strangers, but as she already spoke English she had no trouble adapting and moving into the new space or achieving a good initial job. They settled into a small house, with eleven people, sharing three bedrooms. There were some Brazilians, a German, someone from Japan and a Frenchman. At this moment she realized that she was really alone, but the feeling of being on her own was not as good as she expected.

> When I entered the bedroom he (the landlord) said: "This is where your bed is." I sat down and started to cry. I said: "What am I doing here!? What kind of shit have I decided to do in my life?" Then I cried, cried, cried. Only I have that habit of being very strong... The guys in the house were cool in the beginning, there were some Brazilians that give you tips here and there. They didn't help me much, they said, "Look, the supermarket is there"... They gave some tips about buses, they said, "If you want to save don't get the subway, take a bus"... I started walking alone through the city, the first two months I only walked on my own [Aline].

Aline led a tourist life, she began to enjoy nights out and have some sweethearts. That's when she met a Brazilian guy, Paulo, who was already in London for some time and had a stable life. She began frequenting his house and realized it was time to have a "normal" life, which meant getting a job, especially because her money was running out.

Taking into account these reports it is possible to note that the existence of social contacts and some individual attributes were advantages in the entry and adaptation in the new country; in every trajectory, the same happened at the time of getting a job. Having knowledge of the local language, for example, can open many doors in the beginning, which will facilitate both obtaining better jobs and the mobility of migrants through the new space. These topics will be discussed in the next chapter.

CHAPTER 2

SOCIAL NETWORKS AND WORK

2.1 Getting the first job

I'll start with my case: I was almost a month without work, delivering curricula vitae throughout the city, totalling more than sixty, without any success. I tried to contact the companies on my list of possible employers provided by the Brazilian agency. Indeed, I even tried the pizzeria where a Brazilian friend had worked which also didn't succeed.

As time passed, I became more acquainted with the people I lived with and started to gain their trust. Gradually they began to show solidarity with my situation and began to help me. The first to offer me a job was Ivan. He had a problem with a Brazilian friend who "helped" at parties and was in need of someone to replace her. Ivan wanted me to accompany him at parties and enjoy the party without doing anything else; the only thing I should do was to carry home the money that was the profit from his sales. Usually there were police officers with dogs searching for drugs at the exit, and if he was caught with only the rest of drugs that he didn't succeed in selling, he would be considered just a user and wouldn't have major problems. On the other hand, if he was caught with drugs and too much money, he would be characterized as a drug dealer. Therefore, I would work as "his mule", taking the money home and he would pay me per party. As I still believed in the possibility of getting a less risky job, I didn't accept the offer.

It was through José that I got my first job. I already knew about the S. Cleaner, where many Brazilians worked. Along with other Brazilians, known from school, I went to the company office. We talked to the person responsible (an English woman), who informed us they were not hiring anyone else. And they had no forecast for new registrations. At home, telling my situation to José, he phoned his supervisor at once, also a Brazilian, saying a Brazilian friend, recently arriving from Brazil, really needed to work but still lacked the Insurance Number[13], and the office staff of the company said they were not registering anyone else. Vitoria, the supervisor, directed me to work in attendance at a game the next day and, when the time came to say my name at the entrance of the stadium, I was to use the name Larissa – José's sister-in-law, who had returned to Brazil but still had a record in the company and an open bank account. Upon the payment of the work hours into the account, José would withdraw the money and pay me.

Bernardo, Guilherme, Rose and Priscila, also worked as a cleaner in their first job, yet they did not take long to get it. Bernardo was living in the same house as the Palermo brothers and other Brazilians, who arranged a job for him as a cleaner during the early hours of the morning. In addition, it was through his initial network that (as in the case of the Palermo brothers) Bernardo managed to get all of the necessary false documentation in order to work. He bought an insurance number and a Spanish passport.

The presence of Bernardo in London facilitated the adaptation of Guilherme. Newly arrived in London, he went to the house of his cousin and

13 Social Security card of the country.

This picture was taken in Queensway market (Queensway, Central London, zone 1). The area was know as "Brazilwater", by many Brazilian migrant living there until the early 2000's. The presence of Brazilians in the area is still significant and can be seen by the variety of services offered to the "community" inside of the Queensway Market, such as hairdressers, grocery shops, money transfer services, restaurant and cafes.

they began sharing a bedroom. On the first day his cousin introduced him to the other residents, saying that Guilherme had just arrived and needed to work. As Bernardo had "put his contacts to work" - as he put it - on the second day Guilherme landed his first job.

> I remember that the day I arrived my cousin said: "Tomorrow we are going to buy a mobile phone for you." I didn't want a mobile phone, I can't spend money on phone calls. But he told me: "Old chum, without a mobile phone you don't live in London.' The next day I understood why. We bought the mobile phone and five minutes later a girl who lived with us, and knew I was out of work, called my cousin to say there was a job for me as a dish washer in Soho. Then I understood why it was important to have a mobile phone here, because of the contacts [Guilherme].

Rose's case was different, because she went to live with her brothers and sister-in-law and had already a job arranged for her when she arrived in this English city. She was going to work with them as a cleaner in a restaurant and in a snack bar that served hamburgers. So her first occupation was also subject to the type of work performed by the people of her first home, or to her first contacts in the receiving society. Already on her second day in the city, she had to get up early and get into the routine of the migrant that she wasn't familiar with.

> I arrived in London in the afternoon, the same night we went to the centre, went to a bar, drank and went home. I closed my eyes, and my brother already opened the door: "Hey, hey, let's work, let's work! Good life? Not here. Let's go, let's go." Then I started working in this stinking place as a cleaner [Rose].

Rose worked five hours in the restaurant, from five to ten in the morning, and received £6.50 per hour. As she was not attending the English classes she left this work and went straight to the snack bar with her brother to fry chips. At first it was not too difficult for her to get used to this life, because even though she had to wake up early and do those activities that she never had to do in Brazil, her brother was always by her side helping and protecting her. He always did the heavy lifting for her. Moreover, as she put it, in her work as a cleaner there was no manager "harassing her." She worked in a group of five people, all Brazilians, with the exception of a Colombian friend of her brother: her future boyfriend.

Priscila also arrived in London with a support network already initially structured. She lived in the home of an acquaintance of her friend, rent free, until finding a job, getting one through a friend from Recife, who was already living in London for a longer time. The husband of her friend was a supervisor in a pub, and took her to work as a food runner there, where there were other people from Recife who also worked there because of this Brazilian supervisor. Priscila spoke no English, but as in the pub the customers placed their orders at the counter, her job was just to take the food to the table.

> We arrived at the house and there were only Brazilians there. It was a three-storey house. The first floor is a small brothel, and on

> top it is a normal house. Anyway, we went to live there for two months and I was sleeping in a bedroom with four boys. After we got work, after two weeks, we started to pay [Priscila].

As to Max's adaption, it was more or less different from the beginning because he used his contacts to get help. Hence, he had no intention of keeping in regular contact with those who hadn't helped him to land his first job.

> I couldn't get work because the guys said I didn't speak English, so I couldn't work. It was the only thing I understood, man: "If one cannot speak English, one cannot work"... With two and a half months that I was here I had £5.00 in my pocket, I told my wife that if we could not find work in a week we would go away. I called my friend from Capão and said we needed to work, to help us and such. One of them worked as a cleaner and said he would ask about it at his work. The next day, at night, he called us and said: "Oh, I have a job for your wife, tell her to come to work in such a place at the final stop of the 189 (bus)."At the time I thought: "Thank God it is the 189, because we don't know how to go anywhere else!" She went and met him at Oxford. In the same week her manager, a Portuguese woman, told her to take me there to work too [Max].

Max and his wife went to work cleaning offices overnight. Generally they worked two hours in each building, clearing about four buildings per day, on an eight-hour working day. Max said that the work was simple and fast, they just need to take all trash from the rooms, vacuum the floor, clean the tables, and then clean the bathrooms and kitchen. They earned the minimum wage paid in the country per hour, which was enough to pay their bills and keep on living.

Aline also went to London without wanting much contact with Brazilians in the beginning, although in her first work she also came across Brazilians she met in the city. A guy who studied with her got a job for her in a waitressing agency. From here onwards, Aline got to meet more people and actually enjoyed the life she had always imagined having in another country. It is interesting to note that Aline managed to be a waitress not only because of the contact of her friend, but also because she spoke the necessary English to perform such a task, different from that of most Brazilians coming to London.

2.2. Outlining the cleaning work: The experience as a cleaner

In London, the first work of most of the Brazilians is as a cleaner. Indeed, there is a strong possibility that this work will be in S. Cleaner, a large company that employs many workers, and does not require any fluency in English, especially since the vast majority of workers and supervisors are also Brazilians. As such, the existence of a "Brazilian network" that enables the exchange of information and work recommendation within the company is hardly surprising. Once a contact is achieved within the company, and registration as a worker is made, just a call to the people responsible for "Bucar"[14] (Booking) to find workers for the days when there is an event becomes a reality. To the extent that the network increases within the locations where the company operates, the worker begins to be "bucado" [booked] automatically and the number of shifts that the worker gets can equally increase, provided he/she works hard and has the trust of the supervisors.

The vast majority of jobs that migrants get at S. Cleaner are casual, that is, they work when there is some event and get paid per hour worked without any contract or social protection. The more hours worked, the more the employee will earn. In this context, the workers more established in the company manage to fulfil three consecutive shifts: in the morning before starting, during, and after the event – and regarding the night shift; twelve hours with an hour of rest. Some still do the post-cleaning the next day.

My work at S. Cleaner did not last long, but I started to socialize with several people who worked at the company, since my friend Diego worked there for the whole time we were in London. Therefore, I continued knowing all that was happening in the company and witnessed

14 Bucar is a Brazilianization of the word to book, which means you register, schedule yourself. Words like shift, busy, book, hoover and mop are added to the vocabulary of Brazilians living in London, as if they were part of the Portuguese language.

several stories, such as that of Antônio, the "living dead", as the boys described him, since he worked so much that he hardly slept.

Antonio is a Brazilian man in his forties, who went to Italy with R$ 1000.00 with the intention of spending a year in that country in order to achieve citizenship: non-direct descendants of Italians who live there one year get the necessary documentation. He struggled and, as he said, could only survive with the help of the Brazilian consulate. They found him a little room for him to sleep and endless boxes of pasta during the year. After achieving the desired citizenship, he moved to London to live and work. His intention was to save money and, after a while, bring his family to the UK.

His wife and daughter also worked cleaning the stadiums, but it was Antonio who worked the most. He had another cleaning job, which extended throughout the morning, twelve hours straight (19h - 07h), on top of his five days a week. Sometimes it coincided that he worked during a game – he would do the shift from noon to six - and then he would go straight to another company to do the night shift. People reported that he slept during the two half-hour breaks, in stadiums, when the day's work at the two companies overlapped. Clearly, Antonio worked for twenty consecutive hours. Sadly, this is a very common practice in the case of migrant workers, especially newcomers.

In order to survive such a situation, some workers take *speed* (amphetamine) to enable them to perform their tasks. One day, for example, Diego came home very worried. A boy who worked with him had been caught with drugs by police in front of the stadium that they were going to clean up after a game. A similar case additionally happened with some chefs and waiters of a large events company with whom I had contact. To be able to work double shifts, workers were using cocaine frequently.

Drug use in the workplace has become a practice in many industries where the wage is earned by productivity and/or per hour worked, so the worker can endure the hard work and make more money, as seen in Brazil with rural workers harvesting oranges, sugar cane cutters and truck drivers (FOCOSI, 2009), among which crack use has become commonplace so that they can withstand the pain and fatigue of a hard journey.

In relation to the cleaning work of the stadiums, it took place in a simple and organized manner. People came as workers and supervisors, mostly composed of Brazilians, who were separated into teams to accomplish different roles. There were those responsible for removing garbage from cafeterias, taking the trash outside the stadium; the "hoover" staff who were responsible for vacuuming the carpets of the stadium; and the bathroom staff who were responsible for "*mopar*" [mopping] and cleaning bathroom accessories, such as glasses, hand dryers, toilets, etc. In addition to this main division between teams, the first thing everyone had to do, as soon as the cleaning of the stadium began, was the "pick up" in the stands. The "pick up" was as follows: the worker walked each row, through all the rings of stands in the stadium (with a garbage bag in one hand) to collect objects from the ground, like plastic cups, paper, flags etc. It was very tiring and exhausting work, since the worker had to practically walk two steps and then bend down in order to pick up an object, get up, walk two more steps to another chair and bend down again. Despite being very tiring, it was a job that people still got excited about because often they found money, valuables and even food that fans forgot there. It was common to find some unopened juice or pots with chocolate balls, not entirely consumed that they ate later during the break.

After the "pick up" each team met and carried out their duties until the time of the first break. This usually happened after six hours of work. The break was of approximately half an hour for rest. The workers gathered in the company's room inside the stadium to eat what the staff had collected from the garbage in the cafeterias and would otherwise be thrown away, such as hot dogs, fried chicken, pies etc. Cleaners worked for three more hours and had another 30-minutes break when the time was used to rest their weary body without regard to food.

Besides taking drugs, it was very common for people to get drunk during night shifts, because they had access to snack bars. And, as the stadium was large, some could disappeare for a while to eat and drink in the snack bars, including some supervisors, as I've witnessed. One night, a Brazilian supervisor drank so much that he couldn't walk. I found him lying in one of the bathrooms and he asked me to hide him from the

Picture taken in one of the interviewees living rooms.

English manager because he had already had other problems of this type in the company and could not be caught again. I helped him to sit on one of the toilet seats in the bathroom, closed the door and continued performing my work.

In S. Cleaner one could be working in any event that the company was responsible for the cleaning, for example, in various football stadiums. Perhaps surprisingly, however, the Brazilian supervisors had quarrels between themselves and tried to "take" the scheduled workers to their respective sides. The people with whom I had more contact preferred to work in the C Stadium, which was led by Pedro's team.

Pedro was a 40-year-old Brazilian who came from the ABC Paulista area, was friendly and communicative making people want to be with him just to hear him telling his colourful stories full of slang. Diego always spoke well of Pedro. To Diego he was a nice guy who encouraged people in wanting to work with him, even though in the C Stadium workers were always paid fewer hours than the ones they actually worked. When I met him, I understood why Diego and the other guys liked so much to work with Pedro. When visiting him in the company, I said I was friends with Diego and Carlos, another Brazilian who had worked with Pedro. He soon received me and made me feel "at home". In one of our conversations he told me that he preferred working with Brazilians because the rest of the staff was very slow and didn't work hard, and so whenever he could he would help a Brazilian to work in the company, even when they didn't have the necessary documentation. With this kind of help, it added to the way he built the self-esteem of his employees. Indeed, he strengthened bonds of trust within the company. A speech by Diego expresses well something that I used to hear among company employees:

> I prefer to work in the "C" Stadium than in "A" because there we have Pedro who is always on your side; he follows and values your work. Although you need to work harder in the "C" Stadium, since they use fewer people to do the work and "A" has a lot of people there and you can play dumb and not even work because the supervisors don't care and don't even know who you are. In the "A" Stadium when you get there they already have their preferred workers and that wouldn't change, it was useless to show good service because that didn't change anything. You worked more with Pedro but were rewarded because he could see that you were working. Pedro told me that I 'm on his team and when I work a lot one day he comes and thanks me for the work of the previous day and gives me lighter work to do. He is always praising you and lifting your ego, I know that he is also being cunning but he says that if you work right you will always have work there. On my first day I had not even used the vacuum cleaner yet and he said: "I'm enjoying working with you, huh!?" He could play you so that you wouldn't screw up with him. Like the time I wanted to clean up the event at Silverstone, but Pedro's team was going to Ascot, and

> I felt compelled to go with him because I felt indebted to him, and I didn't want him to take offence [Diego].

It is interesting to note that the relationship between Pedro and his workers refers to what Boltanski and Chiapello (2009) call leaders with vision, those that cause the worker to engage without the use of force, but giving meaning to the work of each one. The manager is seen as the hero of the company, who imposes his authority by charisma and not by status and power. His authority is also based on trust, and since this an acceptable expression of "dominance"; it takes the relationship to a personal level. Adjusting the case studied here, the relationship between Pedro and his workers not only gives a sense of "belonging" to the "unqualified labour" undertaken by these individuals, but also produces an engagement and a sense of bonding: something like "I'm from Pedro's team", a quality of subjective importance if it is related to the precariousness of the relationships established in the context of migration. Unmistakably, the situation of the migrant often resembles what Costa (2004) described as public invisibility, a concept that refers to impaired human perception that is conditioned by the social division of labour, wherein one sees only the function and not the person that exercises it. For Costa, a simple good morning can make the unqualified employee feel that he exists again. Unquestionably, I noticed with the jobs I carried out that courtesy builds co-operation. Indeed, few things were better than a "Good morning" apart from when people referred to me by my name, which was written on the badge.

2.3. Entering the networks and the search for new jobs: Mobility, confidence and control

In almost all the interviews carried out, the first job came from contacts made in the first house. It is a key factor in the process of adaptation and fixation, because in addition to ensuring sustainability, it is often through those sociability networks that life-opportunities for migrants will increase.

Thus, once migrants are familiar with the new space and as their social contacts increase, a greater mobility between jobs will slowly emerge.

Yet how this occurs will also vary depending on the attributes that these workers acquired throughout their professional trajectory, although the simple fact of knowing someone does not automatically give someone mobility. The issue of language, for example, appears in all of the trajectories as something fundamental for improving work prospects. This is especially evident in several trajectories (particularly in the case of Aline) due to the fact that speaking English fluently facilitated her entry into the first job and led to a greater mobility between jobs without relying directly on acquaintances.

To begin with, Aline worked as a waitress in various hotels until 2008; because of the expiration of her visa, she had to return to Brazil. She remained in her homeland for six months, and after a failed attempt to work on a Brazilian cruise ship migrated back to London again: this time Caroline paid for her ticket, someone with whom she had started a relationship before her departure to Brazil.

> Caroline lent me some money to pay for the course (English, to get your visa), £1,500.00. We started a relationship, and I wanted to calm down, I didn't want to go back to work at the agency where I worked before (When I was at the agency Aline went out and drank almost every day with the people from work) [15]. Caroline got me a receptionist job at the Pizzeria and in the mornings I was working in an Italian Cafe [Aline].

Aline felt she needed more work and started to look for work on the internet, since she worked for only a few hours in the Café. She saw a waiter job vacancy in DS an establishment that belonged to a professional society[16]. She sent her resume, and without any recommendation, her interview having gone well, started working there. Eventually, after pushing herself really hard, she became highly valued through the strenuous efforts she made: motivating the company to pay for some

15 Subject that will be discussed in the next chapter: "Extending the stay, experience, consumption, tactics and body."

16 The building had forty bedrooms (to receive members of the society, who traveled to London to attend conferences), a restaurant serving breakfast, lunch and dinner for guests and members, a bar that served sandwiches and drinks, in addition to the events section, when coffee, drinks, and dinner was served to participants.

training and enabling her to become a Team Leader. In itself, this guaranteed many hours of work a week. Thus, she left her other jobs and stayed only in DS. In 2011, she became a supervisor of the restaurant in DS. Aline worked 40 hours a week, with a fixed salary, vacation and all social security rights. She had achieved rapid mobility that few migrants can, and English was in fact one of the differentials in her career trajectory.

The language issue was also important in my personal mobility, even though I was not fluent in English at the beginning. Indeed, I had to go through some other jobs to gain the confidence of those with whom I related in order to get greater mobility, such as acquiring the position of a full time waiter. In this sense, "confidence" refers to the fact that a person recommended for work knows he has the attributes required to meet the needs of the function specified. In addition, this "confidence" also comes from access to information provided by individuals who have had previous experience of working, in this case, with the recommended person. Thus, trust occurs based on knowledge accumulated over previous relationships. This being said, the simple fact of having social intercourse is not enough to guarantee anything, because these interconnections can also be a source of "bad faith" and conflict generation (GRANOVETTER, 2007).

Besides this, the notion of *"confidence"* appears as central in the career trajectory of several people of the cases studied, including mine. As I wasn't established in S. Cleaner and had no guaranteed shifts for all events, I started to look for work around the city. I handed out resumes and did some applications in fast food companies, such as McDonalds and Pret A Manger. Interestingly, the work application forms asked, in addition to some personal data and the reason for wanting to work at this place, if the candidate had been recommended by a worker who was part of the company team. If so, candidates were further asked to provide the name and address of the store where this person worked. As I didn't know anyone, I didn't put any name, which may have been one of the causes for the company not calling me. Equally, I tried some jobs on the Internet. I even attended interviews, but as my English was not good enough I wasn't successful. Once again, landing the second job did not come through my distribution of resumes or applications to companies, but rather through another contact obtained through the house, this time with the help of Rose and Caroline.

Rose lost her first work as a cleaner after she started dating. This was because she started to arrive late every day. Informed by Marta, a Brazilian who did not get along with Rose, Marta told the manager, who dismissed her. What is more, her relationship with her brother deteriorated, since he was the one who had recommended her. Hence, the manager demanded explanations from him as well.

Around this time the situation began to get worse for Rose when her safety net (consisting of her brothers and her boyfriend) began to break down and she had to start "fending for herself" because her brother and sister-in-law decided to return to Brazil, while her boyfriend returned to Colombia. The other brother who had remained in London was living in a house where they had no more room. Still not speaking English, and not knowing many people, Rose moved in with Brazilians, to the house where I was to meet her one month later. At first she had trouble adjusting; people were not polite and didn't talk much with her. According to what Aline said later, the girls of the house were testing her, to see if she could bear staying there or not. Rose also had to be tested and accepted by the locals to get their help. Over time, she was not only accepted but Caroline also got her a job as a kitchen porter at the pizzeria where she worked herself.

However, she was having too much friction with the Brazilians with whom she interacted in the workplace. Adding insult to injury, a conflict with the Australian manager regarding payment developed wherein Rose decided to leave the pizzeria. Fortuitously, she informed me about the vacancy. Strikingly, she warned me that I couldn't get to the place through her nomination. The best way would be to speak directly with the manager, and, if possible, talk to Caroline. Yet she wasn't sure if Caroline would help me, because she was very angry about all the fights involving Rose. As I urgently needed work, I immediately went to the pizzeria. Curiously, the first person I met there was Caroline. I told her about my conversation with Rose. She told me then and there that she would talk with her boss, although I would have to really apply myself, because besides being an unenthusiastic worker, Rose had caused too much confusion and she (Caroline) could not be undermined again. I replied that I would do anything because my money was running out and I'd have to pay rent in two weeks time, and I couldn't support myself with only a few shifts in S. Cleaner. Thankfully, I got the job and as they needed someone immediately, I was going to start working the next day: moreover, I'd be working a double shift.

It was then, through these contacts, that I got my second job in London. It was hard work, especially when I had to do double shifts: the shift began around nine in the morning and ended after midnight. Furthermore, this type of work consisted of cleaning the entire restaurant[17] as soon as I arrived in the morning, and afterwards I was required to clean the whole kitchen, which would be the workspace at the busiest time. Usually I couldn't manage to wash all the cutlery, dishes, glasses and saucepans of the day before, so prior to starting the workday, the morning shift kitchen porter would also washed what was left behind.

Over the next few days I realized there was a tacit agreement between the kitchen porters not to leave a lot of work from their shift for those who would follow after them, or which required a lot of attention the next day. Contrariwise, when they didn't like someone who would start working on the next shift, they dragged their feet in order to leave work behind. Since there were two shifts per day, the first from nine to four and the second from four thirty to eleven at night (the second shift always ended up extending until later, around midnight or 1a.m) this badly affected their co-worker.

Most kitchen porters were women, the chefs[18] were men, and when there was a man working as a kitchen porter, he was soon promoted to kitchen hand, and if he improved his English, most likely he would become chef and would earn more. When I went to work at the pizzeria, the kitchen staff (chefs) were training Rodrigo, a young man from a town in the state of Minas Gerais, who was in London for less than a year, and

17 It was a building with three floors that you needed to sweep and mop the ground of the first two floors, and vacuum the carpet on the third floor. You also had to clean the bathrooms, and wipe the tables.

18 Chefs are cooks who are below the head chef, who manages the kitchen and puts together the menu.

who, from the moment he had arrived, worked as a kitchen porter in the same establishment. Rodrigo talked to me during the first week, saying that the position of kitchen porter was hard work, but as I was a man, I had the chance to become a chef in a very short time.

The working environment in the kitchen of a restaurant is quite sexist and chauvinistic. The women coexist in that space, in most cases, performing only subordinate activities such as washing dishes or at most mincing vegetables for the chefs to prepare the salads. It is extremely hard to find a woman who is head of a kitchen. In this case, gender seems to work also on a characteristic level, both increasing or decreasing the mobility of individuals and directly modifying their trajectory.

Like in S. Cleaner, the pizzeria was paying the minimum salary per hour worked, and employment conditions were poor[19]: five hours of rushing without being able to sit down. The dishes just kept relentlessly coming. Even the waiters took dirty plates to wash and get clean ones to use again. Because they had a privileged position in relation to the cleaners, the waiters pushed them around all the time, asking for "their cutlery" protesting that this process took too long and their customers couldn't wait, especially because the waiters needed to serve speedily in order to gain "tips". Usually, this reached they were allocated a similar amount of money, all received for the punishing hours worked in a day. Yet these tips were never shared with the kitchen staff, a fact which always generated complaints, since everyone was working to serve the same customers, even though only those who served the table got any perks.

The creation of a network of Brazilians working in these pizzerias was well known, especially in the case of kitchen porters and chefs. So, on my first day at work a waitress came up to me and started talking in Portu-

19 The kitchen was located in a small space on the second floor. Only a screen separated the oven and the space in which the chefs worked and the sink to wash dishes and the washing machines for glasses, cutlery and plates. My workspace was tight and, during the working hours of the pizzeria, the pressure was great. As people were eating and dirtying the dishes, I had to take care of washing, drying and polishing the tables, so that they would be ready for the next customers. While the machines washed a lot, someone dried and polished what had just been washed, and because this should be done quickly since the restaurant was always busy, my hands were full of skin rashes and some blisters, because the washing machine used water at a very high temperature and due to the rush we didn't have time to let it cool down.

guese. I found that strange and asked her how she knew I was Brazilian. She said kitchen porters at the Pizzeria were all Brazilians. Because of this, when a new employee arrived on the scene, it is as if there was a need from those already there to inquire into his life in Brazil as an instantaneous icebreaker.

When I started working there I realized that the kitchen staff looked at me with suspicion. Also, they didn't go out of their way to give me much information about the job. They assigned me to work with Rita (aged twenty-eight), a black Brazilian woman from the state of Paraná, who had been in the company for a long time. She was one of the people with whom Rose had caused friction. Rita had to teach me about my workload, but it was clear that she was not very eager to show me how the job was done. Following my intuitions, therefore, I started up a conversation with her to lessen the tension until eventually she noticed that Caroline came to talk to me during working hours. She asked if Caroline had brought me into the Company and if I knew Rose. I had to say I was living with Caroline and that I knew Rose, yes, but I didn't talk much with her because I knew that they had had problems. If I had said, then, that I was a friend of Rose, my workload would probably have been made much harder.

Curiously, not only Rita, but also the chefs started asking me questions about my life in Brazil: what I did, what my parents did, what was the brand of the car my parents owned. At first they liked hinting that I was just a playboy from Brazil, who was there to enjoy life and didn't know what it was like to fend for oneself in the world. However, the fact I worked hard and started telling people a little about my past, made them gradually modify the initial stereotype they had of me.

At this point, I realized that my identity as a child of workers from a town in the state of São Paulo, struggling in London to survive like everyone else, had "triggered" some form of classification. It was from these "interrogations" –that worked more like an initiation ritual, than as real interest in knowing about my life – that kitchen mates started to help me in several ways. Rita began to help me and teach me "tricks" to make the work faster, besides stopping to leave extra dishes for washing when she knew I'd be doing the next shift. Moreover, the chefs came to know what days I went to school during the mornings and that I came straight to the pizzeria without eating anything. And because of that, they made "mistakes" on purpose when making some pizza, so as to leave this "mistake" next to the sink, enabling me to eat something, without the manager noticing, until when it was time for my break.

As time went by, I also won the trust of the waiters, but with them the relationship didn't happen because of my status as a son of a working class family, but due to my student status. Observably, during the break everyone stopped for a meal. It was clear at this point that a distinction was made between the kitchen staff and waiters, since each group sat at their respective tables and there was no visible interaction between them.

One day, as the kitchen staff had already eaten, I sat at the table with the waiters. To feel accepted and seek some identification with that group, it was necessary to use my persona as a sociologist, who was in London to learn English and to earn a Master's Degree. From then on, the way the waiters referred to me during work hours changed; it was as if I started to exist as an individual. I became Junior and not just the kitchen porter.

The person who helped me most was Louise (aged twenty-seven), a middle class woman from Bahia, who married a boyfriend with European citizenship and who intended to live in London, without parental approval, as soon as she graduated from college. Louise was learning English to leave her kitchen porter position. She also did some shifts at another store of the pizzeria, as a waitress. With Louise, I could be myself as a Social Sciences student, without being reproached as bourgeois. Her support went beyond the work at the pizzeria: she gave me advice on how to improve my language skills and get a better job. According to her, if I learnt not to just 'settle' as a kitchen porter, I could get a better job, such as, being a waiter. And, with hindsight, that's exactly what happened.

When I started working at the pizzeria, I had just moved in with Diego into a house with "foreigners". As one of my goals was to learn English, I knew that if I remained living only with Brazilians, learning English would be much harder. It would equally be difficult to get some work that was not on a level with those who lived with me. However, I had become very close to the people in the first house I lived in and still kept in touch with them.

Aware that I was continuing to look for something better and that now my English was improving, Aline contacted me to inform me that there was a vacancy as a waiter at the company where she worked. Her news surprised me, because everyone who lived in the house always aspired to a vacancy there. The DS paid very well[20] and the work was not as hard as a cleaner. Besides, this company had the reputation of being a place where no one was mistreated - since in several companies supervisors and managers treated migrant workers with disrespect and humiliation.

We arranged to meet in front of a underground station because she had spoken with Stan, her manager, about me and I would be introduced to him. Then, we went to the place where the interview was to be held. The building was owned by DS where Aline worked at weekends and where she worked in the restaurant in the morning. Indeed, she was team leader of the waiters in the events section throughout the week. Further, the job that was right for me would be the breakfast shifts on Saturdays and Sundays from 06:30 to 10:30 o'clock.

After personally talking with the breakfast manager, Aline took me up to the events section, where she also worked, to check if *something* could also be arranged for me during the week. However, I didn't know if I would be accepted, because the manager of that department only hired experienced workers.

Norbert was an Australian who managed the events section. Aline introduced me as a friend who had arrived from Brazil a short time before and was looking for work. We talked privately, and he asked about my documents, if I was in the country illegally, and then asked me if I had worked as a waiter before. I spoke the truth, that I had never done that kind of work before, but I really needed to work and would do anything to learn fast. Norbert said he didn't hire people without experience, but as I had been sincere, and most importantly, I was a friend of Aline,

20 They paid £7.50 per hour on weekdays and £10 per hour on weekends.

a person they were very fond of, he would hire me and she would be responsible for teaching me everything. That is how I got my third job, which over time became the only one. As time went by and the managers began to trust my work, I started to get more shifts and finally left the pizzeria.

This trust resulted from my dedication at work. I felt hugely grateful to everyone in my network that this had been recognised. In addition, I now had a moral debt of honour to Aline and Stan for having hired me to serve at the weekends. Thus, I really did everything they asked for, including the cleaning of refrigerators and the floor after breakfast on Sundays, which actually was not my role. Nonetheless, I cleaned up to help Stan. When other workers saw me cleaning the floor or refrigerators, they said I should not do that, that Stan was exploiting me, because I was not the cleaner. Yet even though I knew it wasn't my job, I couldn't say no to him or Aline. In a sense, this also helped me to establish myself more in the company and get more work, especially because I was a worker made pliable through this "bond of trust".

For breakfast, I was a permanent worker on weekends. Shortly afterwards, the company needed someone to cover the breakfast shift during the week and I readily accepted the job. I worked every day, then from 6:30 to 10:30 o'clock, along with Priscila, without any time off in the morning. At least twice a week I replaced Rosangela or Carmina, in the bar when one of them missed work, because Stan had taught me how to handle the coffee machine and the cash register in the bar. In addition, I worked at the events section. The number of jobs was in accordance with the number of events that occurred during the week.

In the events section, employees needed to inform the managers, every Wednesday, about the days and times that they would be available for work the following week. This was because every Friday they would release the roster of the week to come with the names and work schedules of all those required. When the roster was released, the sociologist in me found a situation both interesting and instructive to watch. Everyone expected to see their names as often as possible on that paper because they wanted to "do" the greatest number of hours to earn more money. Those who earned more shifts had prestige in the eyes of other workers. It was as if the shift was a symbolic prize: those who received more hours, theoretically, would be the ones who working better, who strived more. To offer more work to a waiter was a way for the company to reward his effort and dedication.

The workers who had been longest in the company were those who got the most shifts, although the extent to which recent employees had entered the network was also reflected in the fact they were offered extra shifts. That's exactly what happened to me: as I started to socialize more with supervisors, especially after work, and due to always be willing to work without complaining, I started to work at the events section almost every day.

The number of shifts worked then, not only as a reward, but also as a control. If the worker began to cause problems or "drag his feet", this would be reflected in the reduction of work he would get the following week. Moreover, because there was a hidden competition revealed by the allocation of shifts, when workers saw no merit in the number of shifts given to someone deemed unworthy, there was a kind of boycott by the waiters and comments of dissatisfaction began to be heard in the hallways. This situation was clearly illustrated through the case of Lisa, a team leader from New Zealand and one of the best friends of the supervisor who prepared the weekly roster.

Lisa began to leave work and go to a pub with some of the waiters after working hours. It was a rare day in which she didn't get drunk and called sick the day after, usually in the morning, to be excused from work that day. For a while, Evelin - the supervisor who prepared the roster - continued to give several shifts to Lisa who was still missing work in the morning, until the revolt of other workers began to be evident. At this point, Lisa not only stopped getting so many hours of work but also lost her position as a team leader. That is, the ability of Lisa to hold a management position was openly questioned by other workers and managers. Consequently, the trust in her work was lost.

The confidence of a manager in the workplace as well as the mastery of the English language, were also crucial in the ascending career of Max. Unlike many Brazilians, he attended school in his first year and disciplined himself to study. He really wanted to learn to speak that language to "be free" since he felt trapped by failing to communicate with the indigenous population, which was the main reason why he avoided relating to Brazilians outside of the work environment. However, he recalled that his initial mobility, especially when he did not speak English, happened through Brazilians.

Nonetheless, Max's wife got a job as a waitress in a space for events, through a countryman who she had met at school. After working for a month she got an interview for Max who, despite his studying hard, had not yet achieved good English language skills. However, as his wife was a valued worker, the company hired him despite not having the fluency they required, on condition that Max would commit himself more to his studies.

> I only landed the job on account of my ex-wife because she worked well and everyone liked her. On the day the manager told me: "I'll only give you work if you promise to go to school every day." I said: "Man, that's all I want. Work to survive here, and go to school to learn English" [Max].

In order to work more than the hours allowed for students, he bought from a Brazilian an Italian fake document and handed it in the company, so he wouldn't have problems in working so much. During this period, Carlos, a Portuguese company manager, needed help to renew the visa of his boyfriend, a Brazilian who was in the country illegally. As Max was grateful for all the help that Carlos had given him at the beginning of the job, he contacted the man who made his false documentation and got a Portuguese document for Carlos's boyfriend. This act created a bond of trust between him and the manager, who started to help him within the company.

> Carlos asked me to do that for his boyfriend, but one talks to another... I started doing Portuguese documents for everyone. The guy who made the documents wanted to set up a branch there with me in my neighborhood, but I refused; I wasn't here for that. Anyway, it brought me even closer to Carlos; I did him a favor that no one knew, just me and him. He had great trust in me; it created

> a lot of confidence. Man, he taught me everything I know today about events. So I started to grow within the company, because at that time I didn't want to go back to Brazil, I wanted to grow within the company, because I wanted to stay in London [Max].

As Max was dedicated to learning the local language, his English improved rapidly. Moreover, he felt gratitude for people giving him the job even without really speaking English, which made him work extra hard. As a result of this hard work, and a closer relationship with the Events Manager, Max, who had achieved the position of waiter in September 2003, had been promoted, by March 2004 to the role of Team Leader. He says the fact that he became friends with Carlos helped him in his work. However, this rise was not only due to the simple fact of knowing the manager, but equally due to his hard work and the trust that Carlos placed in him.

> I grew within the company through my work, not because of my friendship with Carlos. I got my job, I learned, I did my job well, with his help in teaching me. I then grew within the company. He helped me by teaching me how to do the work. So, he helped me. Not directly, directly! Because if I didn't work well I couldn't progress and besides that the bosses were very demanding. So you need also to trust the person, it is not enough just knowing someone, because that person can create problems for you at work [Max].

Max claimed he had recommended, as well as helped, a number of people in his years of living in London, but always made sure that he could trust the person involved. Likewise Aline[21] also told me that she had only recommended me for the work in DS because Caroline commented that I worked well and she could trust me. They both, perhaps especially Max, relied on information from people who had worked with them that such and such a person could be trusted for a particular job.

21 "Because you spoke English, and I didn't want to get burnt. I didn't want to recommend a person who didn't speak English, or a person who could get into trouble, and Caroline had told me you were working well at the pizzeria, everybody liked you, and you related well with everyone... Ah, I didn't want to mix things" [Aline saying the reason why she recommended me to the work and not the others in the house].

Moreover, if this person had already experienced problems elsewhere, neither of them would help in order not to get "burnt" themselves.

> Everywhere I've worked I just took people I knew I could trust. Not that I knew I could trust, but the guy came already from another job, people had spoken well of him to me, I had information. Type: "The guy works fucking well" then I would arrange it. Furthermore, only the fact that the guy was an acquaintance of mine wouldn't be enough for me to take him on. Like Jessica (current girlfriend), she turns and says to me: "Dude, I have a friend there, from the church, from the house where I lived, she is in need of work, arrange work for her here." I always say: "Baby, people I don't know I don't place them here." Vandão (brother-in-law who went to live in London with Max's sister in 2009) for instance, I won't arrange for him to work with me in DS. Why? He doesn't speak English, and I know he will be hard work. Bernardo (Brazilian who shares a house with Max) is always asking me to place him there, but I don't, because the guy has a bit of a temper, he is a troglodyte, will get into fights and will burn me. So I don't. Cíntia, a girl who lived at my home, nice girl, honest girl, good girl, works well, she asked, I said: "You took your time; they are in need of people at my work." I took her straight away, she spoke with the director there and he took her on the spot [Max].

In 2004, Max's visa was expiring and his wife wanted to go back. So Max went to Brazil and took his Portuguese citizenship to live in London again. As his wife did not want to spend the rest of her life *there*, Max told her that they would return to England, would work and eventually buy a house in Brazil. When the house was built, they would return to their homeland.

As he had already lived a year in London, on his return in 2005, things were easier. He and his wife returned to work at the same events company, and were living in a house with Brazilians who they managed to meet through contacts with friends.

> I wanted to come back to live here, but my wife wanted to save money to build our home there in Brazil. We wanted to go back,

> because here was much easier to save money. Then my friend from Capão who lived there in the building where I live and he got me a place there in Bernardo's apartment. So we arrived here already with a place to stay, and work was easy too. I called the staff where I worked and said, "I returned from Brazil now, I arrived here and I want to work." I arrived here on Saturday; on Monday I got back to work [Max].

Max and his wife went back to work at their previous company and soon he became a manager again. Yet, as the value of the pound was high in comparison to the Brazilian *real*, in a short time they built the house and his wife began to press him to return home. Once again, he returned against his will. Tellingly, their situation deteriorated when he began to feel pressured by his wife's parents who appeared to want to control the couple's lives. Max lived in Brazil from October 2006 to April 2007, when he returned to London, albeit single. As such, he went to live in Bernardo's apartment. At that time he didn't want his old managerial job at the events company. Instead, he wanted to make progress in London and started a business in the construction field with a Greek friend whom he had met at the time when he worked at the events company. As Max said, he always tried not to have many relationships with Brazilians, despite always having received help from them when he needed it. In part, this was due to the perceived fact of suspecting that Brazilians were always "pulling" something on someone - like Rose, Priscila, Aline, and many others whom I interviewed, had narrated. Furthermore, Max always wanted to grow job-wise, and if he stayed only with Brazilians he would have the same lifestyle they lived: being a cleaner, a kitchen porter or a waiter at the most. For Max, Brazilians lived all together doing the same kinds of unqualified labour.

In this way, Max tried to establish ties outside of the "Brazilian networks" that would serve to help achieving some professional mobility in London, but as he always said, if the contact was important, even harder must be the work. Without this, no one could achieve anything. Thus, it was by his drive to "get ahead", added to his accessing information obtained by non-Brazilian acquaintances, company mates and so on, that he held down good jobs in the city.

Indeed, he applied himself to work with his Greek friend for a construction company they themselves had opened. They worked together throughout the year 2008, and earned a lot of money. Nevertheless, by the end of the year Max went back to Brazil on vacation and stayed from December to March, placing company business to one side. According to him, his friend couldn't manage the company during these three months away, causing his business partner to break up the firm since, apparently, he spent a lot of money and poorly managed affairs.

When Max returned from vacation, he did not stay long without work for long, because once again he got information through the contacts he had made with top management in the events company where he had worked previously. Cartman, a Canadian who was a marketing director for the company, had gone to perform the same function in another business, DS, and when he learned that Max was looking for employment, invited him to work in DS., although, he would not act now in the role of manager. This position, after all, was already occupied. Nonetheless, Cartman said to Max that with his resume, he would quickly progress.

Indeed, Max worked hard and achieved a high position in DS. Accordingly, he sought to meet the expectations of those who had trusted him and finally reached a prominent role. He obtained in 2010 a fixed contract with the company, working 40 hours a week as a manager.

In the case of Rose, who got into fights, added to the fact that she didn't speak English, it meant that people who related to her didn't feel confident to recommend her for some jobs, which often limited greater mobility in her career trajectory. Following the fights, she went through difficult times when she was out of work. She no longer had the boyfriend to support her and the brothers to help her out. Moreover, no one else in the house where we lived wanted to help her because Caroline had said that Rose was not reliable and had quarrelled with everyone in the pizzeria, causing her problems because she had recommended her. So, in a way, Rose was "socially dead" in the circles of sociability that she had built until then and would have to start from scratch once again.

To further worsen a situation that was already difficult, she lost her job in early December, 2008, exactly when the market in "unqualified" work, that is, the market of migrant workers, was stationary. This was due to the fact that hiring for the holiday season had already been undertaken and, it being winter, the number of events and festivals had severely reduced. She looked for work for a month, throughout the city, and found nothing, until she decided to try again to re-establish the lost ties with those who had helped her in the beginning.

> I decided to try the cleaner job that I did when I arrived in London. I called the manager, and said: "Barbara, how are you? It is Rose, look I'm calling you to ask for employment, to return as a cleaner. Now I'm educated to London life, I'm more responsible, I'm used to this life of London. I'm unemployed, I would love to work, I really need a job." And she said: "Okay, come back in February." I went back on the fifth day of February. When I returned, I vowed, I gave myself three months maximum for me to go to classes, learn the basics of English and look for another job [Rose].

Rose returned to work in January 2009 cleaning a restaurant late at night. She began attending English classes, and searching for a place to live with foreigners, because that way she would have to speak English. During this period she got an Australian boyfriend for a while, which also helped to improve her fluency in the local language.

During these three months, the period which Rose had given herself to learn English and get a better job, her brother began working at the restaurant and laboured at dawn as a runner. From the entry of her brother into the company, Rose managed to work as a runner in the restaurant during the hours of serving meals, and later she remained to clean the toilets of the same restaurant, which turned into a sort of nightclub during the early hours.

Because Rose had to raise the money needed to renew her visa (that was due to expire at the end of 2009), the thirty hours of work she performed was not sufficient to support herself and still pay for the visa. Therefore, she tried a few other occupations and, with her improving English language skills, got some shifts through an agency for waiters. One of these positions was in DS, for a few days, and as Aline worked there, she called Aline to ask if there was a vacancy for her too.

> I always asked her (Aline) and she always said that there weren't any vacancies. She didn't recommend me because she didn't trust me. It's because Caroline used to say that I was a troublemaker,and that I get into fights with everybody. But really. Man, because when I'm right I really speak up, but I'm humble enough to apologize, to say: "Damn it, I am sorry." And after all, this is something normal at work [Rose].

In fact Rose was right, Aline told me, on the day that I interviewed her, that she didn't trust Rose due to her having caused problems for Caroline in the pizzeria.

> I didn't want to bring Rose to work here. She mixes things up. And about Rose, Caroline told me, "Oh, be careful, think twice, you are really going to hire Rose?" She caused trouble for Caroline in the pizzeria, and eventually she came on her own. I actually wanted to avoid trouble for myself, that's all. And at work I am like that, I am really very professional. I don't like to mix things up, because otherwise, you tend to really protect that person because she is your friend, and I don't want to do that. I just brought you because you speak English, and I didn't want to get burnt. I didn't want to place a person who didn't speak English, or a person who would stir up trouble, and Caroline had told me you were working well in the pizzeria, and that everybody liked you, and you related well with everyone [Aline].

As Rose realized that Aline was not sure about possible problems in recommending her for work, she waited for Aline to go on vacation and delivered her resume to DS in person.

> I went there, I looked for Norbert (Australian manager of the events section) and he was on vacation. I went there in front of the restaurant to talk with Núria (Spanish restaurant manager). I arrived speaking English, but I felt that she spoke Spanish, so I started to speak Spanish, but she continued in English. I said: "Oh shit, what do I speak, English or Spanish? Ah, I will continue in Spanish." And in the end, I finished off with English, all mixed up. I said: "Because I have come here to bring my resume. I've worked

> here through an agency. And I'm looking for a job. I would love to come back, really." I didn't say that I was a friend of Aline, I didn't say anything [Rose].

She left her resume and after a while, to her surprise, she received a call from the events manager asking her to attend an interview. It was then that she used her *social capital* and said to Norbert that she was a friend of Aline's. Only when Aline returned from vacation did she find out that Rose had gone there for an interview and had talked with the manager saying she was her friend. Rose was hired and started to work during breakfast under the supervision of Aline. As they needed someone to do someone else's shift who had missed work, the managers called her because she needed money for the visa renewal.

About a year later, speaking even better English and established in the company, Rose was tired of working in a restaurant; she really wanted to work in a clothes store. As she didn't know anyone who worked in the area, she found it very difficult to get a job.

> What I wanted to do here, I wanted to work at a store called All Saints. I love that store, I have sent my resume twice and they haven't called me and I tried other stores and they didn't call me too. I felt so disappointed, so hurt, so hurt that I didn't succeed. Why here I cannot get work in a store and in Brazil I don't need to send a resume! Ah, of course, everything is about contact, my love, everything here is "who will recommend" you. Even to be a cleaner you need a recommendation from someone, here or anywhere in the world, anywhere in the world. How did I land the job in the Pizzeria? Caroline placed me there. How did I become a cleaner? - My brother. How did I work in Hamburger? My brother placed me there. I get so angry, I'm like: "Shit, I have to stay in this shit polishing plates" [Rose].

As Rose said, and their other trajectories demonstrate, social contacts are important to intermediate mobility between jobs. However, the attributes of each person will vary according to how these contacts are or are not used, including some and excluding others. Besides the importance of language, as it has already been said, there is also the "paperwork" issue, because those who do not have legal documents in this country will have a greater "dependence" on social networks, which they utilize to get work and to acquire false documentation. This dependence often cannot only limit the mobility of an migrant but also be used as a form of exploitation. This happened with Bernardo.

Because Bernardo was working for a few hours, cleaning offices during the early hours, one of the Palermo brothers, an events manager on a cricket field, took Bernardo to his work in an attempt to get some work for him. As he didn't speak English and had no documentation, they agreed that Bernardo could work at the stadium, provided it was for free for a while, as a test. He started by organizing the drinks and filling the fridges with beer. As he urgently needed to speak the English language, the Brazilians who worked there - many by the way - made a list of basic terms in English, which were necessary vocabulary items that he should verbalize so that his employers wouldn't realize that he didn't understand every day speech.

> They said: "Oh Bernardo, you have to do this." The work there is called backhouse. And they left me a sheet of paper there to study, so that when I was asked for things I would know what they were. He showed me on the sheet: "Oh when the guy asks 'where do you come from', you reply 'I'm from Brazil', or what is your name... Memorize: "how are you and what's your name" because they will ask, it is the first thing they ask. I arrived: there at noon, the manager came up to me and said: "How are you?" and I said, very excited: "I'm from Brazil." The guy went mad saying: "Fuck, fuck off." After the guy saw that I was working hard there. But I didn't know any English or the work. He called a Brazilian and said: "Ask him what else he can do?" I said: "I do anything, I'm here to work" [Bernardo].

Due to being a hard worker they tried to place him in another sector, but he was also lost, since he understood nothing of what was said to him. The manager was watching everything and had tried to help him again, taking him to work in another sector, which also didn't work out.

> He (the manager) said: "Oh, you are unable to work here." Then I

> said to the Brazilian guy there: "Tell him that he will not stay here either." He already kicked me out of the job. He said: "But I have an opportunity for him, tell him that I bought a new house and if he wants to live with me, he will learn English. But he will have to build some things in the house for me... Does he know about building work?" I said: "Ah, I do know." I lived with this guy for almost a year and it was in his house that I learned a little English [Bernardo].

Bernardo moved in with the manager of the cricket ground and his family. The manager was English, married to a Polish woman and had a couple of small children. Bernardo lived in the attic of the house, had food and shelter, but did not receive any money from the family. The little money he earned was paid by the cricket stadium, since he continued to have a work record with the company and the manager punched his time card for him every few days so that he would receive a little money.

> It was a shit at first, I hated it. When it was morning, seven o'clock in the morning, I woke up in the guy's house; I had to wake up, and the guy was there. He used to come to me so early in the morning, and say: "Good morning" in English. I had to talk just like him, but I could not. And at night time: "Good night, how are you?" He was trying to teach me, and I was mad because the guy was talking to me. I wanted to be alone, I didn't understand anything. He would come, open a wine and say: "Come and drink wine." I would say: "No, I don't drink." It was just so I wouldn't have to stay with the guy, but I was eager to drink the wine [Bernardo].

As time passed Bernardo started to come out in the house and learn English, mainly because their son spent the entire day at home watching Bernardo work and teaching him English.

> I lived on the top floor of the house, and they had a little boy who liked me a lot, and when I worked the little boy went there and kept saying the names of things. He pointed at things and said: "Pigeon, pigeon, airplane". That's where my English improved, I learned a lot with the little boy. I started to see them as my family. And they liked me. They once had a nanny from the Czech

> Republic, and I was making out with her, they found out; they fired the woman and kept me there. They were always giving me advice. They always said: "Do this... do not try to mix with these people, do this..." they were always giving me advice and I was always going in the wrong direction. One thing I learned from my mother, do not take shit from anybody, then, my brother, I really strike back. In the stadium I've fought three times, because the Brazilians there are envious of me, jealousy and such... they kept talking shit, but I don't leave things alone. The family calls me bad boy, but they like me very much [Bernardo].

He lived with this family for a year and with another Polish guy who also worked with him in building the house. He was getting up at seven in the morning and worked all day, every day of the week, including Sundays. He only had Saturday night off, and it was when he went to the house of the Palermo brothers and spent the night drinking with the Brazilians.

When he finished the house, as the manager knew that Bernardo was undocumented, he took him back to work in the cricket ground, but now with better English than when he had arrived at the stadium for the first time. As much as Bernardo had been "exploited" by the manager (such as the typical cases that we have in Brazil of traditional families that take children to live with the family, wherein the mother becomes the house maid on the pretext of providing food and shelter to children), Bernardo also did not feel exploited, and saw this as a symbolic exchange: hard work was what he could do in gratitude for the work and the house that he had been given at a time when he had nothing and nobody.

The feeling of gratitude to the English manager was so great that Bernardo said nobody helped him more than the Englishman, not even the Brazilians. This reflected on his work at the stadium. Max said that the staff at the stadium exploited Bernardo, that he worked hard, did everything for everybody and was still paid less than what he was legally entitled to, because he was undocumented. Max knew this because, when he was not yet a manager in DS, he worked as a waiter at some games, in the cricket stadium.

As work at the stadium did not last the whole year, only when there were seasonal games, Bernardo started looking for a second job for when work at the stadium stopped. At that time, he wanted to save money to bring over his girlfriend who he had left him in Brazil. He asked the owner of the apartment where he currently lived, if someone was in need of some work. The owner of the apartment "hired" him to organize the office of his real estate business, and then to paint some apartments that he had bought. As he had no experience, and depended on that work, once again he accepted being "exploited" to obtain gains from contacts he was making, and worked for free for three months, as a test, and when he began to receive money he didn't earn the same as the other painters.

> The guy said: "What can you do, paint?" I said: "I can." I painted a house and the guys went and had a look at it. They liked, but didn't say anything because he used me for three months. I did everything perfect. But the guys exploited me... because nowadays you earn more than £1000.00 to paint a house... And the guys paid me £ 300.00. And the work is very hard. Just what I needed! Because I was at the stadium only a few hours and I wanted to bring over my girlfriend that I had left in Brazil. Besides, the real estate guy also sponsored me; he got work for my girlfriend when she arrived, so I kept still painting the house for him, even though I was being exploited [Bernardo].

The sponsorship of the real estate owner "worked"; in addition to the work for his girlfriend, he also got a third job for Bernardo, in order to keep them in London. Thus, he also began working in the early hours at a hotel bar. At first he didn't understand what the customers were requesting, but as he always served them generous doses, everyone liked him and helped him. As there were no Brazilians working in this hotel, Bernardo managed further to improve his English.

> I started working in this hotel in Notting Hill, in the bar. With the English skills I had it was a comedy, bro! I didn't understand anything... the guys would come and say: "Give me that", I smiled and looked at the guy, the guy "that one there", "This?" "No", I would take one and say: "Not this one, this here? Okay, how much?" The guy smiled at me, I filled the glass. When I put less the guys com-

> plained, I put more, the guys would leave a tip, I must have caused a loss for the bar. But I was learning and had a staff that cared for me and helped me with English. There was an old couple who lived in Notting Hill, they had no son or anything, and they went there just to see me and drink. They made me read the newspaper every day; every day I read a piece of the paper. They laughed, the old lady said: "You will learn English this way." [Bernardo]

As he spent all day working, his girlfriend started complaining of the life they led in London, she didn't like working as a cleaner and complained all day that she didn't see him.

> I had to get out of the cricket ground and to help my girlfriend who was pissing me off. In reality she was a "girl who was born with a silver spoon in her mouth" and suddenly became poor for nothing, because her father had money, but he left her mother who was a crazy woman and left the two of them broke. I ended up bringing her here, but she didn't want to work cleaning things. And she was upset and I was already upset with her too, because she didn't want to study, didn't want to do anything and stayed home all day. I came home broke, she was sad, I asked her what it was and she said that the account due date of her mother was getting close; I went and paid the bill for her mother and she was happy but two days later she was sulking again [Bernardo].

As they were fighting a lot, Bernardo left his bedroom, which had a computer, TV, fridge and a double bed, and split a bedroom with another Brazilian who lived there. Meanwhile she became involved with people from an Arabic church. Then one day she said she was leaving and taking everything, including the fridge.

> One day she said: "I'm moving out today", I said: "Okay". I was in my bedroom, I went to her bedroom, I knocked, and said: "Oh, you're moving today? Okay. Then I want to do some *shit* to you. What I did for you until today you are going to forget, but wise up!" I slapped her right in the middle of her mouth, she fell to the ground, and I said: "But this here you won't forget, will you?" She fell to the ground, turned purple, came at me, and scratched my

> face. I gave her a good punch. Everyone in the house tried to hold me, and I was saying: "Don't hold me, that's all I want." She started talking again and I slapped her pretty hard. Everybody was scared. Someone in the building called the police [Bernardo].

Bernardo fled and didn't turn up at the house for some time and his girlfriend filed no complaint because she was also undocumented. According to Bernardo, she did the "passport swindle" already the following month and married an Arab who had European citizenship.

After this episode, Bernardo returned to his bedroom but had to buy all his stuff again, as she had taken everything away. Over time, he returned to work in the cricket ground. The manager had found a way to get him back in the company, even with a false passport. After that he worked in the cricket ground until the end of 2010, when he had another fight at work. However, in February 2011, he said he had already talked to the manager and would work in another section.

Bernardo spent, therefore, much of his time in London circling the jobs he landed with his initial contacts, specifically limiting himself to work at the stadium and often being exploited by those who got him the work. Learning English didn't give him a very high mobility, since the issue of the documentation continually limited a greater leap.

The trajectory of Guilherme mirrored that of Bernardo's in several aspects. Both had similar beginnings in London and came from a similar origin. However, over the years, Guilherme began looking for ways to escape the precarious lifestyle of an undocumented migrant.

In his first job Guilherme realized he was being exploited by his boss, who only hired undocumented migrants so that he did not have to pay the minimum wage.

> It was a nice environment, all Latin, Bolivian and Columbian people. The owner was a Spanish exploiter. He was an old exploiter, who hired illegal staff so he would pay only half. He paid exactly half. I worked eight hours, then earned £150.00 per week when I should earn 290, 300. But for those who were up to a week at a pet-

> rol station in Brazil, and experienced all I did to enter here, it was good! Then again, we ate there and the food was good. I started at four p.m. and left at midnight. I had a day off in the week... My cousin took me to the guy there, a Brazilian, to get the false documentation, get what you need to work and such, because I wanted to get another job [Guilherme].

When Bernardo went with his cousin to get his documentation, he learned that the Brazilian man who sold the documents was married to a Brazilian woman, who was the manager of a cleaning company. Guilherme was offered work at the company. However, he would need a passport, insurance number and a Portuguese identity card. Guilherme bought the documents and began to work at the company during the early hours cleaning offices. Over time he found out that the couple only hired undocumented migrants to exploit them. This was for two reasons: they were earning money selling false documentation to the workers they employed and were only paying cleaners half of what the company transferred to them for their salaries. As Guilherme still felt grateful for being given work, he accepted the work conditions and began his second job.

> Dude, I worked for three months in the morning cleaning. It was fucked because I was leaving the restaurant at midnight, got home about one in the morning, took a shower, and my cousin was always home, we always talked. I went to bed around three in the morning. And I started cleaning at six in the morning. I had to leave home at five a.m. [Guilherme].

Tired of the abuse and hard work in the restaurant, he started working at another restaurant, which belonged to an Italian. It was a job achieved through information obtained through colleagues at the cleaning company. Despite also being exploited at the Italian restaurant, since he was receiving less than minimum wage[22], he remained there because the

22 "At that restaurant the worker wasn't paid per hour but per shift. So I was exploited there as well, because I did two shifts that were like from 9:00 to 15:00 o'clock, however I never left at 15:00, I always stayed much longer, and the other shift was from 17:00 to 23:00 o'clock that went also until one in the morning, and the guy didn't pay any extra" (Guilherme)

job was easier. Later on he worked in four other Italian restaurants, and since he interacted with Italians on a daily basis for two years, he ended up learning how to speak Italian.

Due to the lack of legal documentation, Guilherme had to be subjected to various other jobs in which he received half of the minimum wage, such as a restaurant outside London, where he worked in 2009, when I first met him. He got up early, spent more than an hour travelling, worked all day with only a thirty minutes break without food, and only one day off per week. Many days he had to sleep in the restaurant as he finished work late (after midnight) and public transportation wasn't available following this time. After two years of washing dishes, Guilherme got a job as a kitchen hand in a restaurant through a friend who shared a house with him where they paid better wages. However, this wasn't permanent work.

Like Max, Guilherme knew that if he remained socialising only with Brazilians his mobility would be limited. When he said that to me, I asked him to explain further, since he had also said he couldn't live in London without having contact with Brazilians. That's when he explained, practically giving me a lesson from his experience, about the idea of homophily and its consequences in the practical life of individuals[23].

> If you want to progress here you need to learn English. But, do you remember I told you that you could not be here without a

23 Homophily is the tendency that individuals have to build and maintain contacts frequently with individuals of similar social characteristics (McPherson et al., 2001; MARQUES, 2010), i.e., it is produced by intrinsic dimensions of sociability, such as practices, taste and language. In the case of international migration, what can unite these individuals initially is the same origin of migration, but despite this sociability "among equals" helps in finding jobs and occupations, and access to care and companionship (social support), it also ends up serving as a social control for some. This can hinder possible social mobility for these individuals, since they do not relate to those who have different attributes that act as bridges to mediate access to new goods and services (BRIGGS, 2003; 2005; MARQUES, 2010). It is import to highlight that the mere contact with different individuals does not necessarily generate an active social capital, i.e., it doesn't necessarily produce a sense of community or connection patterns between groups that will bring gains to individuals (MARQUES, ditto). However, there is no denying the fact that staying in a relationship only with your primary group reduces the possibility of having greater mobility.

> mobile phone?! That is because of contacts with Brazilians. There is one thing that is like this; if you stay a lot in the middle of Brazilians, you will not learn to speak English here, which is true. However if you don't engage with Brazilians in the beginning, you don't get a job. It is Brazilians who will get you a job, it is not an Englishman, or Japanese, or a Danish guy... And if you are, like in my case, here illegally, who will get you the documents to work? It is a Brazilian! False documents are with Brazilians; everything that you may need. If you are going to drive a motorcycle, car and van, who is going to get this driving license for you? A Brazilian. Who will put you in the job market of the vans, the couriers? It is a Brazilian. Who will put you in a restaurant to wash dishes? It is a Brazilian. Who will put you in cleaning to clean floors—a Brazilian. You learn where the cheapest places to live are, where it is more worthwhile living. "Ah, such or such a store is having a sale promotion!" "Change your mobile phone, because more people use that brand, that mobile carrier." It's all Brazilians. Hence you meet people and move on, Dude. If you are going to study later, you decide. Then, later, when you already see that you can get by on your own and want to leap higher, you have to go for it. I have this vision. I think Brazilians live too much in a ghetto... They live in the ghetto and don't get out of there. If you want to get out there what you have to do is to leave the Brazilians. And that's when I changed my life here Dude, because I already had two years in London and was living this little life, and I saw many people, working as a kitchen chef, in construction, and earning much more than me. I thought: "I cannot stay here the way I am doing" [Guilherme].

From this change of thinking, Guilherme began to look for jobs where he would have to speak English. He wanted to work as a chef, but he couldn't cook even an egg. Guilherme was always asking his cousin to get him a job in the cricket stadium, knowing that they had a kitchen there and he could start working helping the chefs. However, he felt that his cousin did not trust him very much and was always making up stories to avoid offering him a job. For instance, Bernardo gave the excuse of saying that the Home Office regularly raided the stadium and he was not caught because the staff warned him and he was able to run out the back.

As he continued without a steady job, Guilherme began to run out of money, so decided to buy and sell false documents:

> Some acquaintances wanted to get documents and I started to refer them to the guy who did them. Only after a while, a lot of people started asking, so I started to add my share so I could earn some money too. But a guy who did business with me was arrested and he was in the newspaper. The guy (who was arrested) came to London and started this scheme to make false documents, to clone cards and such. And you know how it is. He begins to make easy money, and go to parties, women... The guy was picking up Danish, Norwegian women. It went to his head...Drugs, drink, nightclubs, limousines…It went to his head and this one is now in jail. He had parties at his house, took photos at home with money on his chest, and put the picture on Facebook with the Norwegian women and the money…Anyway, so it ended up becoming dangerous so I got out of this business… I was starting a new lifestyle [Guilherme].

With his new lifestyle Guilherme started his new job. Although his cousin had said that he could not work at the stadium because the Home Office always raided there, he ended up getting a job there through another friend. As there were many people from his Brazilian city living in London, one day by chance he met a former neighbour of his, walking in the city centre of London. This friend said he had been in London for some time and worked in the same stadium that Bernardo worked in. Guilherme asked if it was true about the Home Office and his friend said he had already been working illegally in the stadium for two years and had never heard of this. After this information, Guilherme told the story to Bernardo and said he wanted to work in the kitchen of the stadium starting as a kitchen porter.

The next day Bernardo spoke with the kitchen chef, told him about his cousin saying that despite not speaking English, he was a very hard worker and would like to work as a kitchen porter. The boss told Bernardo to take his cousin there the next day to start working. However, when they arrived, Guilherme had a surprise.

> I arrived there; the guy (boss) looked at me and laughed. I was wearing a shirt of my football team Santos, so he asked: "Oh, what team is this?" I understood and answered: "It's a team from Brazil." The guy was English and supported Chelsea, and he started saying: "Santos is shit, Chelsea is much better." That guy turned out of nowhere and said: "You will not work washing dishes; you will help me in the kitchen." I felt desperate... I thought: "I'm fucked; now the guy has caught me, I don't know English and I cannot cook right." I turned to him and tried to say: "No, I will not, no, I want to wash dishes; I don't speak English." He said no, that he liked me and that I could understand him, that I would learn little by little... So I went! [Guilherme]

For Guilherme, this moment, which happened in 2010, was the extra step that he aimed for: he was receiving the minimum wage for the first time and would be forced to speak and practice English in the kitchen.

> It was my time to leave the ghetto in order to grow, because I have more prospects for growth. I started there as a sub chef, who is one category below the chef. So I was there, helping the chef, but I was washing dishes no longer. Also, I got the minimum salary now! And there I was punching the time card when I started and when I finished; then the hours I worked were the amount of hours I got paid. Not to mention that I was learning to speak English! In the beginning there was an Australian guy who was the son of an Italian, then I spoke to him in Italian. This helped me because when I didn't understand something, he would translate into Italian to me. But after four months he left, and from then on it was really only English [Guilherme].

Guilherme saw in this work his opportunity to improve his life in London, so he started to work hard, never complained about anything and he did everything that he was asked to do. He said that this made everyone like him because usually working in the kitchen as a chef's assistant is very hard work and the staff always complain.

> Dude, it was my chance ... I said: "I'm going to work hard!" On the first day they gave me three hundred pounds of potatoes to

> "*pilar*"[24]. I had never done anything like that before, I thought I wouldn't manage. I remember that I started in the morning, at seven o'clock in the morning until eight at night and I finished the next day at noon. I thought: "Man, I'm very bad, one day and a half to do a job! And the place where I worked was a reputable place; it was the "Maracanã"[25] of the cricket." And the guys were watching me. Two days later, they gave me more to "*pilar*", and something else, and the comments started: "Gee, this guy is enjoying that." I thought: "I don't believe it!" [Guilherme]

As he was a hard worker, Guilherme began to hear positive comments about him, which made him proud and gave him more strength to continue working. Even Bernardo, who was previously reluctant to take him to work at the stadium, said the chef thanked him for taking his cousin and that he earned respect within the company because the boss asked him if there was anyone else reliable that he would recommend.

Priscila also felt exploited by those who arranged her work at the beginning and only achieved higher mobility when she learned English and began to move and live in other circles.

After a few weeks of working in her first job, in a pub, Priscila had to leave the house where she lived, as she was only allowed to stay until finding work. Since she was already working and met more people, she soon got another place to live with her co-workers. However, she still moved house a number of times afterwards because she found out that she paid more rent than the other tenants in both houses. After finding this out, she could no longer trust any Brazilians, because to her, the vast majority thought only of money and taking advantage of others.

This was also one of the reasons that motivated her to leave the job in the pub. She was working several hours a week, above the national allowance for students, without having to show a work visa, due to the fact that the manager was a friend. However, this "easiness" provided via social contacts, or networks, had a price that had to be paid.

24 Brazilianization of the word "peel", that in Portuguese means to peel.
25 Brazil's famous Maracanã Stadium in Rio de Janeiro

> I left the pub because I was tired of the place, because you worked and you never get paid. You took vacations and your money was never there, you know? Like, your hours were always wrong and you would complain and he never fixed it and I was tired of working for free. To work for free is not on, every week, and an hour or two less. After a month, you've got millions of hours less, in two months you already have a billion hours less, in three months you'll already be working more for free than receiving any money [Priscila].

Priscila always knew that they were paying her less than her entitlement. Yet, as she could work at the pub more than the twenty hours legally allowed, and as she didn't speak English, which would allow her to get a better job, she continued working in the pub for another two years. She always knew learning English was important in finding a better job so she tried to attend classes during her first two years in London. When she realized that she already knew many people in town and she felt more confident with respect to the language she decided to look for a new job. Through the help of her classmates, she started working as a waitress in a bar inside a luxury clothing store. Despite only having a student visa, Priscila also worked more than twenty hours per week at the bar, but didn't get paid properly.

Afterwards, through the recommendation of a colleague, Priscila started to work for a waitressing agency belonging to a Brazilian woman, the same agency where Rose worked occasionally. It was at this agency that she heard about DS, as the company often used waitresses from the agency at big events. The agency staff received £5.50 per hour working at the DS, since the agency kept £2.00 per hour from each waitress. Learning this, she left the agency and asked for work in the DS restaurant, who paid £7.50 per hour, where she was accepted in early 2009. For the first time in London, Priscila found a job without a personal reference and earned above the minimum wage.

The amount of information presented in this chapter cause some theoretical considerations to be addressed. The way mobility within a working environment is developed, in each trajectory presented, explains that contacts actually enable access to privileged information. However, the network acts as a mediator and not as a Producer. Both social relations and attributes are crucial in this process (MARQUES, 2010), because the

This picture was taken in central London near Soho. This area of London is very well known for its live entertainment, large number of resturants and pulsing nightlife. Many immigrants work in the area providing the sort of service that they themselves have been accustomed to, for many a pertinent reason for staying in London.

simple fact of knowing and relating with someone does not guarantee the access to opportunities, unless they also have the social characteristics necessary to have this access; and in the cases described here, one important feature is the demand for English language skills.

Knowledge of the local language opens many doors and provides greater mobility. It is, to an migrant, not only a differential in workplace mobility, but also in the way they live. Language is primordial in moving around the city and understanding the culture. Those who do not have access to this are left out of some circles, such as networks for jobs, local culture and news media (Knowles and Harper, 2009). Thus, they cannot access information outside the primary group. Those who do not speak the local language will always seek to live and work with Brazilians. Their social networks will be composed of Brazilians, that is, most likely they will only have access to that information and other types of work that other Brazilians have. Hence, their experiences are lived in Portuguese and lost in translation; they shut themselves away and interact only with a few people. Thus, an important variable in the migrant adaptability debate is knowledge of the local language.

Another important point refers to the idea of trust. To have access to certain goods and services arranged by the networks, these individual must be trustworthy. In this sense, the idea of merit is constantly present and, all the time, each worker is being assessed by those who make the links. An individual only introduces another into a specific place, provided there is high level confidence that indicates a person will correspond to the requirements needed to perform the job. On top of this, they must have the attributes necessary for the practice of that function, and of course, be willing to do it without causing any trouble. When expectations are broken, it is not only the individual who has let the side down, so to speak, who will become discredited by others, but also the credibility of the one who recommends them in the first instance may be called into question. As a consequence, the ties of "network connections", which are based on such "confidence" may become "loose". This happened to Rose several times.

When the opposite happens, where the expectations on the person appointed are fulfilled, the one who appointed the employee also obtains symbolic gains. This means that the action of the one who recommends someone to the job is not completely altruistic, and may be of interest to them (Mattedi, 2005), as they will gain prestige and trust within the company. This situation happened with Aline in DS when she recommended me and also with Bernardo when he recommended Guilherme. The ethos of 'trust' is a finely tuned barometer, which acts as a precarious dynamic in a migrant's pathway.

Guilherme's speech demonstrated how the idea of altruistic people was not really present among *brazucas* (Brazilians) who live in the "land of the Queen", and that self- interest was also present in actions considered altruistic.

> So it follows that the idea that Brazilians help each other here is a kind of legend, dude; a kind of legend. You help because you need to be helped, not because you are a good guy, oh no. Like, did the guy go to receive

> me in Spain? No fucking way. When he saw that I had nothing to give in return, he didn't turn up. Do people help you in the beginning? They help, arrange documents and such, but it is also because they are going to gain from you, sometimes even exploit you [Guilherme].

This comment, like several others heard in the field, makes us relativize the idea of ethnic solidarity among Brazilians in London (LIGHT, 2000), such as it has been analysed by studies with Brazilians in the U.S. and Canada (MARTES, 2003; GOZA, 2003). In those places, there are also cases of exploitation carried out by Brazilians on other Brazilians within the so-called "solidarity networks". This takes place mostly when the migrant has no documentation becoming more dependent on this "solidarity network".

Furthermore, as demonstrated by Lima and Conserva (2006), even though networks make it possible to gain access to inside information, they may also, depending on its intensity, function as an element of discipline for workers. More specifically, at the same time that these social contacts may function as a "capital", which allows individuals to enjoy the advantages offered by such a relationship, they may also result in social control through the rules and sanctions from which the group, or community, can be benefited, such as inhibition to crime or behaviours considered harmful to the community, or to the company (LIMA and MOURA, 2005).

Taking this discussion specifically to the labour market, Boltanski and Chiapello (2009) claim that reciprocity is no longer in the exchange of objects, but rather in establishing links, which are a capital that doesn't belong to the one who enjoys them, it can always be replaced unilaterally, in the form of punishment, by the one with whom it was created.

Thus, the way the networks of relationships in the labour market is established would be, for these authors, the new "manager" in the company, and this control would come through the trust that ensures the link between the "actors"; it is the trust within social relations which unites all the members of the company. Trust cannot be broken, all stakeholders, workers and managers are responsible for it; they are responsible for their behaviour, that will maintain or not the trust (and work) that was given to them. This became evident in all cases presented, especially in the situation where Lisa lost her position as a team leader in DS.

CHAPTER 3

EXTENDING THE STAY: EXPERIENCES, CONSUMPTION, TACTICS AND BODY

3.1 The eagerness for work and the lifestyle.

As noted from the descriptions above, newly arrived migrants, when established in a job, will have an initial devotion to that job, working as many hours as possible, always trying their best to avoid disappointing those who employed them. This happens not only with those who go to London with the initial intention of working-saving-returning, but also with those who theoretically would be students, as in the case of Rose, Priscila and I.

When I settled in the DS I worked up to seventeen hours per day. This was further intensified when Stan asked me to work in another building (DS 2) part of the same company on weekends. So I started working all day Saturday as well. During this time I worked up to eighty hours a week, always with Max, as the managers said we 'didn't drag our feet' in front of our supervisors.

We began to work hard as well as party a lot. When we worked on weddings in DS 2, we started in the morning, around 9:00 am, and went until 1:00 am the following morning. As soon as we finished work, we always met with some friends and went to a nightclub or a pub. There were days when we went out at night and had to be at work the next day for the breakfast shift. On these occasions we worked "straight"; we went home only to shower and change our clothes to begin another day of work. So I ended up engaging in a rhythm of living marked by hard work, consumption and travel. I bought several electrical goods and travelled to eleven different countries within Europe. In the same way Aline and Rose also became "enchanted" with the lifestyle they led in London, juggling work and social life; attending English school became secondary.

> "I started working and I was sent to work in various hotels in the beginning. And with all this I was also studying. I always did my work schedules according to the school. But I started working, meeting people from employment agencies. They were mainly Brazilian people. And at a hotel I met some girls, you know? They were very nice girls. One was Luciana, who became a great friend. And Luciana had always been very crazy, like, she knew everyone and talked to everyone, and wanted to take me all over the place. I went! I moved house, I moved to a place on top of a pub. So everyone used to go to my house; we drank, drank, and drank. We went on a spree. I quite enjoyed it. I partied a lot. Then the networks increased... And people meet this way [Aline].

It was then that Aline realized that her life was being summed up by parties and work as she was no longer attending English school. After a while she moved into the home of her friend Luciana, where she would meet Caroline, her girlfriend.

Until then, Aline was still experiencing a period of partying and discovery. She had never kissed a woman before but said she already felt like it. Over time, she was sleeping with Pedro, going out with Luciana and something had already started with Caroline. Taking into consideration the lifestyle she led in Rio de Janeiro, Aline was entering into a phase of new experiences, and those experiences were easy to be lived out in London. Yet, her student visa would soon expire and she would have to return to Brazil for her sister's wedding. She had never planned on staying more than a year outside of Brazil, but the "enchantment" with the "free" lifestyle that she had led, eventually became one of the reasons to come back to London, especially for the sexual freedom she had away from her family.

> I had never been with a woman. But I left Brazil with this idea ... I said to myself: "It is now that I'm going to hook up with a woman." I felt like it; I thought this was normal. It was normal behaviour and that in reality everyone, deep down, had a same-sex attraction, and I said: "That will not classify me as a homosexual", I think that's normal. And it was impossible to happen in Brazil because I did not frequent gay places. My friends didn't know anyone gay and such. And if I talked about that to a friend of mine, I don't know how the person would react. Then, I had this prejudice. But when I came here, I was on my own, it's different. I went after someone [Aline].

Aline tasted, in London, the freedom that she sought so much in Brazil. When she returned to her parents' home she felt like a 'fish out of water' and felt too different to live again as before. The situation got worse when her sister told her parents that Aline was a lesbian.

> The sexual issue was a very strong thing. It got stuck in my head. I said: I have to solve it again. So I said: "Oh, you know what? I need to go away again. I'll spend six months working on a ship until my head is back in place." It means, in reality, my quest was always for freedom. I wanted to feel well with myself, to sort out my head and be at peace. I really decided to leave when my sister saw my conversation with Caroline on MSN, on a social networking program, and told my parents that I am a lesbian. My father and my mother pretended not to hear. I left home, I went back two days later and my mother did not speak with me properly until things

> settled down. They never asked me anything, so I also left it quiet. But the atmosphere became uncomfortable [Aline].

In an attempt to once again escape from family pressures, she began to arrange to go back to London. After six months of staying in Brazil, she returned to London in February 2008, this time to stay for a longer period. As Caroline had lent her the money to go back, Aline moved in with her, already as a couple.

Rose also experienced a situation of changing her initial migration project due to her lifestyle in London. She worked up to ninety hours a week spending too much on travel and binge drinking. Despite having planned to stay only one year in London, Rose also wanted to save money to renew her student visa, as she didn't want to return the Brazil again so soon.

> Man, I worked so hard and went out so much, I did so many things ... I used a lot of drugs, I tried cocaine, took ecstasy, LSD, MDMA, ketamine. Wow, I tried all kinds of drugs, took ecstasy, and sucked one here and another there in the bathroom. I was very crazy; it was the craziest year of my life. Wow, I fucked a lot, I drank too much... I even hooked up with women ... But I hated it [Rose].

Priscila, although she did not go out as much as Aline and Rose, had also fallen in love with the free lifestyle. Away from her family she decided to renew her visa and extend her stay. She started doing many hours of work, and similar to many others, she left school and worked increasingly harder, despite not having the intention of saving to send money to relatives who were in Brazil. The money saved was going to be used to renew her visa, which would keep her for a while longer in a life free from family pressure, providing her the opportunity of consuming a "cultural life" that she didn't have in Brazil.

> I was attending school because of the visa, but as time passed, I got a few more hours work in the pub, and started doing forty, fifty hours, and they kept increasing. I left the cleaning job; I stayed only at school and at the pub. But I also missed school a lot, as I didn't have the patience to go there; I only went sometimes because of the visa [Priscila].

Many of those who move abroad with the initial thought of learning English for a short period, end up having certain experiences that make them decide to stay in the country for a longer period of time. The school was no longer a priority, as in the case of Rose, Aline and Priscila. However, this did not happen only amongst those who migrated as English language students. The majority of interviewees who migrated in order to work and earn money for a short period of time stayed longer than they planned, and didn't know for sure when they would return to Brazil.

If hard work was the key to ensuring a "free life" away from the family for the three women interviewed, in the case of Guilherme, Bernardo and Max, the initial idea of working hard to ensure a "future" in Brazil was replaced by a longer period of residence in the UK, given the ease of local consumption.

As seen earlier, Max migrated with the initial goal of learning English. After a year in London, realizing how easy it was to earn money, he returned to Brazil, took his Portuguese documentation and returned to London with his wife to save money to buy a house in Brazil. They worked together for two years, bought the house and went back home. Max could not readapt to the lifestyle in Brazil and missed the life he had acquired in London, which was strongly marked by a safety and ease of consumption that he didn't have in Brazil.

> Her father (the wife's) would phone and they cried together like children. I already wanted to stay here and settle for good; I didn't want to leave. Because, Dude, beyond the issue of purchasing power that I mentioned to you, there is also the issue of violence that matters too. Because here, you walk down the street and don't expect to be shot at any time, you don't expect that two guys fighting in the street will exchange shots and a bullet may hit you. I already told you the story... My brother was shot in Capão Redondo and died. My other brother was also shot in Capão Redondo but thank God he didn't die. So there is all that. Everything counts, Man, it is like my mother says: "I cry every day longing for you (for him and his sister who went to London in 2009 with her husband and two children), but I want you to stay where you are because the violence here is very great" [Max].

Max returned to England after a year. At that time, when I first met him, he worked up to 90 hours a week to be able to buy electronic products, which he couldn't purchase in Brazil.

> I like it here because of the purchasing power that money has. We work and get worn out, but you get more stuff. You have an ease of obtaining things pretty fast. For example, I bought a camera for £850.00. You can buy this camera in one month. In Brazil, only the camera's body, without lens, costs R$ 6000.00. It's much easier to take £800.00 from your budget here than R$ 6000.00 in Brazil. In Brazil, working as a waiter you would never manage to buy a camera like this. I used to get pissed off for cleaning other people's shit but there was an incentive with the purchasing power that money has over here. In a month you pay for a ticket to Brazil, £800.00 pounds, and every year I go to Brazil and I pay £800.00 for the ticket. By working here for a month you can afford an overseas ticket. In Brazil if you work for a month you don't pay for an overseas ticket to spend a month's vacation in London. So, Dude, here I can live the present, today, now; in Brazil it is more difficult, you need to be planning things and paying things in installments [Max].

As for Bernardo and Guilherme, since the beginning they went to London with the idea of the economic migrant who just works, doesn't eat, doesn't sleep and doesn't spend any money, but as time went on, they also started to change their life goals and length of stay in the city.

Guilherme says that his initial idea was to work hard, not spend money on anything, save it and return to Brazil within four years. It was what he tried to do especially in the first and beginning of the second year. However, over time his initial idea and his lifestyle began to change.

> When I came to London, I didn't know how to turn a computer on. I had only a mobile phone in Brazil, because my work required one in order to schedule overtime; if it wasn't for that reason, I'd never have had a mobile phone. The idea one gets when coming over here is that you'll stay four or five years and you cannot drink

> a coke because it is expensive; you have to save without going out, without spending anything. That was the initial idea, stay for four or five years, save as much money as you can manage, send it gradually to Brazil and then go back. There was that idea of guys who go to Japan, they don't eat, don't sleep. I thought it was like that here too... Until then I didn't know how to handle anything (electronics) and now I have a lot of stuff here, computer, mobile phone, TV, clothes... Yep! I never had this idea of owning all those things, ever. Living here things start to change; your mind changes a lot [Guilherme].

The high purchasing power and ease of consumption that offer Bernardo a lifestyle that he wouldn't be able to have in Brazil, also made him change his initial migration project, in which he stopped working hard in order to return to Brazil.

> The life that I have here I'll never have over there. I bought a Kawasaki Ninja (motorcycle) with a salary and a half, which costs R$ 35000.00 in Brazil. Like, a house there costs seventy, eighty thousand, and you build it to stay there all your life paying the mortgage in instalments. Here, in the space of one month, you buy a lot of things, everybody knows that, that's the reality; that is the reason why everyone comes here and stops thinking of going back. Today I was talking to Martha at church. She is a woman, over forty years old, she told me she lives in a room with her two daughters, lives badly, everyone cramped, but they have everything. She said she will never go back to Brazil; she is here illegally, but the church people have said they are going to help her out. Here they have everything and her daughters are thrilled with life here. If you want you can cook a steak on the hot plate every day, drink a beer. There you have to buy sausage. Even working as a cleaner you can have all that here. [Bernardo]

As the initial migration projects are revisited, these migrants must find ways to stay longer in the country, without running too many risks. It is within this context that some survival and permanence tactics emerge.

3.2 Survival tactics and permanence: the folds of legal, illegal and illicit[26].

This initial enchantment with the lifestyle amongst Brazilians performing un-skilled jobs in London, is common. Several of those who came to the city with the initial idea of studying English, eventually stopped attending classes in order to do more shifts and make more money. This allowed them to obtain a "passport" for entry to this lifestyle, which they began to value. So many of these "students" whom I interacted with had already been in London for either a few months, or years, and didn't speak any of the local language, even when they stated that their initial goal was to learn English.

The student visa was a very lucrative business for language schools in the city. Many individuals who wanted to spend time in London had to pay a school to facilitate their entry with a tourist visa. However, there was a register of attendance carried out by the Home Office[27] in which schools were required to pass on student attendance to them, weekly, and if the student was not attending classes, they would lose their student visa.

As a result, many schools, at that time, besides charging fees for the courses students took, earned extra money by charging a "fine" for missing classes. When they noticed that a student missed too many classes, a letter was sent to the student advising them to go to the school to "regularize" the situation otherwise the student would become "illegal" within the country. Yet, when students went to the school, many school directors offered a "deal": the student could pay to remove documented absences.

Something similar happened to me when I started working many hours a week. Although I was not working a large number of hours in

26 I use the term tactic following the idea of De Certeau (1994), for which tactic would be the art of the weak, a calculated action, a movement within the field of view of the enemy and the space controlled by it. He operates blow by blow, move by move. He enjoys occasions and his bases depend on them to stock benefits, increase ownership and provide outputs. That is, they are skilled gestures of the "weak" in the order established by the "strong", it is the art of giving blows in another's field, a cunning of hunters.

27 British Immigration Department

order to "survive", but rather to maintain a lifestyle of partying and travelling, to which I had entered, I became involved with the logic of "work hard, play hard". Like many others, I started working more hours and had no time to attend classes. Also, I spoke English at work as well as in the house where I was living at that time; my pronunciation had greatly improved and I didn't feel it was beneficial for me to attend classes. If I had any questions I clarified them with an Australian girl who was living in my house (later she became my girlfriend). As a result, I stopped going to school and I received a letter from them requesting me to attend or I would become an "illegal" in the country.

Prior to going to the school I called Caliban, an English language teacher who had become a great friend. Caliban was my first teacher in London, and when I needed to miss a class in order to work, he always registered my attendance. However, when I changed classes the other teachers I had didn't do the same. Consequently, I had too many absent marks and so received the letter. Caliban reassured me on the phone telling me to calm down, because, most likely, the director would propose a deal and I would have to pay a few pounds to get rid of the school absences. As Caliban said, the owner of the school just wanted to make a lot of money from migrants, paying the teachers badly and didn't care whether or not a student was learning the language. I told him that I didn't have much money saved at that time because I had just paid the monthly bills and I would only get paid at work the next week. That was when Caliban remembered that I had not yet taken the thirty days of leave to which I was entitled, and that I could negotiate that with the director.

When I arrived at the school, everything happened exactly as Caliban had said. The director pressured me, saying that I was in the country illegally and could be deported at any time. This would make any migrant feel terrified and be ready to accept any proposal he would make to put an end to the situation. When he finished speaking, I asked, following Caliban's instructions, if there was anything that could be done to prevent my deportation. The director asked openly for £300.00 to erase the twenty-seven absences that I had. That's when I told him that if there were only twenty-seven absences, I would like him to swap these absences for my holiday entitlement to which I was entitled. Although he didn't like my request, the director accepted my proposal, charging me £20.00 to cover the "administrative expenses". Upon leaving the director's office I went straight to the school office to request them to place me in the class in which Caliban taught in the evening. From that day on, my bond of friendship with Caliban facilitated my life: when I couldn't attend classes, there wouldn't be any absences recorded.

A similar situation happened with Rose. She stopped attending English classes to work as she was saving money to pay for another English course and to renew her visa. Rose was always complaining about her school; she used to say that it was very bad and that the teachers weren't even English, they were Brazilian. This became another reason for her to not attend classes and work harder to renew her visa. When she tried to do so, she discovered that she would need an attendance letter as well as a progress letter showing her level of English obtained at the school. As she hadn't attended classes, she didn't make any progress, so the owner of the school offered her the letters necessary for that renewal, if she continued studying at the school.

Driven by convenience and need, Rose paid for another course at the same school and renewed her visa for another year. Nevertheless, the school served more as a trade for visas than as an educational centre. For this reason, the Home Office sent a letter to students telling them that the school would be closed down. Rose went to school and found out that she would need to pay for a course at another school to get her visa again. She would need the same two letters as before, but this time she had to pay £600.00 to get them.

These cases were repeated frequently in 2009. Several acquaintances of mine paid schools to achieve the necessary school attendance. However, when I was still there, the Home Office began investigating and pressuring schools about irregularities. Many of these schools have closed down and since then if a student misses classes over a five-day period the supervisory body will become notified. The hour's students were allowed to work was also cut from twenty hours per week to ten, in 2010. In 2011 students were not longer allowed to work. These measures were taken to reduce the number of "illegal"

This picture was taken in an area long established as an entertainment district, with numerous sex shops and 'services' to offer.

migrants in the country, especially in a context of economic crisis. In developed countries, it appears to some that the blame always falls on migrants.

That stated, even though barriers were designed to "hinder" the stay of migrants in London, migrants develop tactics of "survival", along the porosities between the thin barrier of legal and illegal, sometimes even using "illegal" means to maintain a situation of "legality".

Priscila, for example, also made use of illegal practices: she paid for letters from her school to stay in the country "legally". When I interviewed her in 2011, she was keen to make her visa status legal because there were rumours in DM that she was an undocumented migrant. Priscila showed me all the money spent on visa renewals, courses that she had paid for and didn't need to attend and letters of class attendance. Furthermore, she told me something that she had never told anyone because she felt ashamed about it: to get money at the end of 2009, when the restaurant of DM was closed for renovation and she was out of work for three months, she again crossed the existing folds between legal, illegal and illicit.

She needed to find a new job, as soon as possible, since she no longer had any money saved and needed to renew her visa. Her Brazilian network arranged access to a job that she said she would have never done in Brazil; she started working as a receptionist in a brothel. Although she was not a prostitute, she felt the burden of moral weight that falls on the sex industry.

> I was in need of work. In the house where I had lived in, there was a girl named Rafaela. I thought she did a few odd jobs and not what she said she did. She said she was a cleaner but she left the house looking tidy and returned looking tidy. Her clothing was never dirty, she had a fixed schedule, she never had a boss, never commented on anything about cleaning, she didn't translate the word cleaning[28]... Damn it, she didn't do any cleaning. There were never any stains on her clothes like a person who does cleaning. I was at that time without the work of DS, and one day she came into my room and told me she wanted to tell me what she did, but she didn't want me to tell anyone else in the house [Priscila].

Rafaela told her she worked in a brothel, offering her a job for a few days.

> She came and said: "I came to ask if you want to do something, if you want to work where I work, you know..." I turned around thinking: "Now she is going to tell me what she does." I said: "No,

28 Usually when people start working in the field of cleaning they don't use the terms in Portuguese but rather the terms in English like 'cleaning' and 'cleaner'.

> because I know that you work as a cleaner" and she said: "No, I work in a massage parlour." Until then I thought it was really a massage parlour. She said she worked at the reception answering phone calls, and I could work there as well and all I need to know was the price of things. And I said: "But what about the language? How do I say in English 'face exfoliation and other things about the face'? And she said: "No, the person calls, you say how much it is, and there will be a list there with the price of everything, and over time you will know the name of the things, you read them. It's easy, after they get there, and they pay before entering the bedroom." I looked at her and said: "They enter the bedroom? What do you mean, Rafaela?" She said: "No, they enter the bedroom and stay there with the girl." I looked at her sharply: "Rafaela, it is a whorehouse then." She said: "It is." And I said: "Then don't tell me that is a fucking massage parlour! So do you work in a whorehouse?" She said: "Yes." "Oh, okay, so I don't need to know about exfoliating or anything, right?" She said: "No, no...". "Oh, yeah, so now we're talking the same language." She told me how everything worked there. I asked: "And what about the police? Any police raids?" She said": "They might have, but from the moment they arrive there, you take your shoes off... you go to work with a nice outfit and take a pair of flip flops. If the police shows up you're a call girl too." I said: "But I don't want to be a call girl." "Priscila, if you're a call girl it is better than being a madam, because if you are a madam, you're selling the girls and you'll be arrested. It doesn't matter if the money is not for you, it is you who is serving customers and getting the money, so for the police you are the owner. So from that moment on, you put your flip flops on and pretend you are a call girl." [Priscila]

As she needed the job, Priscila accepted. The owner of the house where she got the job was a Brazilian woman who had been a call girl in London for a long time and ended up opening, with her husband, their own "house". At the house all the girls were Brazilian, but they didn't say they were Brazilian to the customers, because Brazilian girls were very popular in this business, and if word got out, the house would get too many customers and would become more visible to the police. It was a normal house, furnished with a living room, computer and sofa. Priscila was a sort of concierge in a space inside the room, along with a security guard, who was also Brazilian. She answered the phone and spoke with the customers, receiving the money from them, when they arrived, and she was responsible for paying the girls at the end of the day.

> The guy would call, and I would say: "Oh, there are two girls." You never said they were Brazilians. "She is Spanish and so on. They have a bust with that many inches, butt, she is blonde/brunette." I sold them, as if they were a commodity. When the doorbell would ring outside, I had to look at the camera, through the television, go there, open the door and then they would enter. Then I had to go up to the bedrooms' corridor with him, the girls would stay at the door, in their panties, bra and robe. The customer would see the girls, choose one and tell me what he was going to do, what he wanted, because he would pay me upfront. When the house closed at night, I divided the money between the girls and took my share [Priscila].

Overall, the customer had to pay the minimum of £40.00 for twenty minutes, in which he was entitled to only one ejaculation. This value gave no right to anal or oral sex. If the customer wanted this type of service, he would pay an extra amount that was agreed directly with the girl. The sum of money the girls earned was very flexible, as it depended very much on the week being busy or not. Priscila said that on average they earned £800.00 a week: an amount already with the discount of 50% since they had to pay the owner of the house. If a woman made £500.00 in one day, she would take home £250.00. Priscila received £70.00 for a twelve hours shift and the security guard received £50.00 to work from 9pm until 2am. The workers usually worked twelve hours, from 2pm until 2am. Over time, Priscila ended up being part of this network, working within other brothels, as was the case with the workers. As customers didn't always like being with the same girls, the owners of the houses passed on their contacts to other owners, also Brazilians, who invariably phoned them offering work. Priscila worked in four houses simultaneously. Moreover, there was an entirely informal market that circulated around this "industry" and this market also consisted of Brazilians.

> Everyone was Brazilian, but they were girls from here that called to find out about work or opened our door wondering if we were

> in need of girls and such. But mostly it was someone who already worked there and took a new friend. And there was a lot of Brazilians who went there to sell things to us. It was always people who would sell food, candy, jewellery, panties and bras. They arrived there in the afternoon and sold things to us, I myself have bought jewellery from these Brazilian informal importers [Priscila].

Priscila said she was lucky because the police never showed up while she worked there. If that happened, she thought she would have not put the "flip flops" on to pretend she was a call girl. Although she knew it was foolish, she didn't want the police to look at her and think she was "that"; she didn't want to be seen like "them" because she would feel dirty, like the girls. She would rather be arrested than be labelled a whore. She recounted the stories she experienced in the job, disgusted at being a part of it, and when I asked if she thought this kind of job would be like any other, she became upset.

> No! It's a worse job because what I learned about them there is that it is not just getting there and opening the legs. It is not. Firstly, it is not easy to spread my legs to someone I don't like. There are all kinds of people, it is a black guy that you have to serve, it's an ass that you have to serve, it is a whiner that you have to serve, it is a stinky guy that you have to serve, and there is more; the guy does the way he wants and you have to accept, you have to accept everything, like, pretty much everything, and I saw that they didn't like it. Even the type of work I was doing made me feel uncomfortable. If it was in Brazil, I would never do it. Sometimes it's as if here it wasn't my reality. But although I was not doing anything wrong, just answering phone calls and opening/closing the door, I was in a dirty environment. Once Junior, (security guy in one of the houses) told me that, because as he lived near me he took me home every day, we used to arrive about two-thirty in the morning. I'd never commented anything of that business being something dirty. But he commented: "Priscila, when you get home, you have to take a sponge bath?" And I said: "I have to take a bath before bed." He asked me why. "The reason is that if I don't, I don't wash off that filthy slime of that disgusting environment off me." He said: "I feel the same thing." I said: "Bullshit, do you feel

> the same? You're a man." He turned to me and said: "Yeah, but I try to take a shower because otherwise I can't sleep." I said: "Yeah, but I'm a woman. Do you feel the same?" "I do feel the same. That environment, everything, is all over me. It is on my clothes, it is on me." But I was a woman and I thought that I was the only one to feel it, but he told me he also felt the same [Priscila].

Priscila also said that this was a very insecure environment, which could be violent. Junior, the security guard whom she talked about, had been stabbed three times by customers who caused disturbances with the girls. Nevertheless, Priscila said that many Brazilian girls, from a better or worse background – whether they were thin, fat, white, or black – were still doing this kind of work in London, and all the girls she met at the several houses where she worked in, were not being forced nor had gone to London just to do this work. The circumstances of their lives had led them to this kind of work, which is often more profitable than washing toilets and serving people in restaurants. Priscila equally told the story of a girl who became her friend and who, like the vast majority of those who are there, began to prostitute herself as it was a way to earn money quickly.

> Camila is younger than me, she is from Sao Paulo, but her mother lives in Recife. She is twenty years old and has a very beautiful body. She came over here because her uncle sexually abused her. She came to London and worked at Starbucks making coffee. She said she was tired of Starbucks at the time; she worked hard, had to stand all day, her legs tired a lot and all those things. Then she met some girls who worked in prostitution and earned a lot, and she saw that she worked hard and earned very little, and she began working as a prostitute. Nowadays she works only three days a week, because she went back to Starbucks. She's well, she has an English boyfriend who doesn't know what she does, of course. She said she's trying to quit, has cut down the days of work in the week, but is still making some extra money three days a week. But she was always complaining to me, she used to say: "My life sucks, and one day we will die, go below the soil, and I need money, my mother doesn't help me at all, and she only can say to people when I arrive in Brazil that I'm beautiful, that I'm many things, I'm not

> sure what and show me off to everyone feeling great and showing that I'm such a hottie, and arranges my hair." Like, she is really hot but her mother doesn't even know that she was abused by her uncle from seven to fifteen years of age. So their life is also not so splendid [Priscila].

Priscila stopped working as a prostitute when the police came looking for girls who were being forcibly prostituted. No one was arrested because what they really wanted was to find girls that were being trafficked. Priscila wasn't there at the time the police arrived, but feeling the danger getting closer, she realized that she didn't need that job and she quit. She went back to DS three months later once the renovation was completed.

The work in these houses helped Priscila to find another tactic, which allowed her to stay in London without having to renew her visa and pay for courses. A friend told her that some Brazilian lawyers in London could get a visa without the need for payment: when I last met her she was checking whether this was actually possible.

> I went after this Brazilian lawyer, who was recommended by a friend of mine. I said I wanted to stay until the end of the year or even next year and what I could do without having to attend classes. He said to me: "Priscila, I can request that your visa be extended, the visa you already have. And you will not pay for another course, you won't need to attend another school, and you don't even need to have money in your account to prove that you are able to support yourself here." He filed this application for extension, I paid him £2,000, but he said that if I wanted he would get me to stay for about five years by stalling the system. He said that is the way it works: "It is unlikely that they will grant you the visa. It is more likely that they will deny. But I'm going to appeal with another justification that they will probably deny. But I'll appeal with a justification that will take a long time to be resolved, to win time. So they will deny it again and I'll appeal again, so I guarantee you five years here in the country." Soon I received this letter (she shows the letter), saying that I'm waiting for my visa, so I am still legal here [Priscila].

The lack of having a visa may make it difficult to get a job, or as observed earlier, it facilitates subjection and exploitation, given that when workers don't possess documentation they are exposed to high levels of abuse and humiliation, performing long working hours and getting paid below the minimum wage. To escape this situation, various tactics are used, such as buying a fake passport, a driver's license and an insurance number. I often met people who had such documentation, such as Guilherme and Bernardo. Even Max, before obtaining his Portuguese passport, used a false Italian ID in order to work more than the twenty hours allowed.

The practice of buying a passport is commonplace among undocumented Brazilians, and prices vary according to the similarity to the original and how many people are involved in the business network. The greater the number of intermediaries, the greater the price to be paid, as Guilherme explains:

> Prices vary according to the quality of the paper and the number of people who get involved, because everyone wants to get a cut. My document is Portuguese, you pay £300.00. A driver's license will cost you £70.00. An Insurance Number, which is like the Brazilian CPF, is cheap: £20.00 or £30.00. Now if you want a "hot one", which is hard to get here in England, you will pay about €3000.00 if there aren't a large number of people involved. It works like this: there is a Brazilian contact here that has a contact there in Italy. He takes this Italian guy and gets an Italian passport and sells it to you. But he sells it to the guy there in Italy for €1000.00. This contact sells to a Brazilian for €2000.00 and this Brazilian guy sells sell it to you for €3000.00. If there are more people involved, the passport is more expensive. This passport must have the guy's name, now in the false passport, like mine, you can put any name you like. I put my name, but the date of birth has been changed, name of parents has been changed and the birthplace has been changed. You do whatever you want, put the data you want. I put my name so as not to confuse myself. Because the guy turns around and says: "Martin", talking to me, and I'll stay there watching without knowing that it is with me [Guilherme].

Picture taken in the corridor of an interviewees house

In 2010, Guilherme learned of another trick that would guarantee him to stay legally in London. As he had already re-thought about staying longer in the country, he started seeking ways to be legalized. They told him he could find a foreigner who was older to register him as his son, since he had not been registered by his father in Brazil. This way he could get European nationality and everything would be easier, as he could visit his family in Brazil whenever he wanted.

Guilherme did not have to look far for a European "father" as he had seen an advertisement in a Brazilian newspaper in London. He paid £5000.00 (spending all his savings) requested by an Italian "father" and the record became made in Brazil. However, he needed more money to go to Italy, stay there for a period of time and obtain the necessary documentation. So, he was saving money to go to Italy but eventually he discovered that in Italian law, currently, the person recognized to be a father had only a year to file the application for citizenship and that time had elapsed. Consequently, Guilherme contacted someone in Brazil who managed to change the record date. More money was spent, which was not a problem for Guilherme because, as he said, his goal was now to acquire citizenship since he wanted to stay for a longer period in London.

Another very common practice for achieving permanent residency is arranged or purchased marriages. I once went to a party of Brazilians with Max, where I met some Brazilians who had been in London for over a year. Their visas would soon expire and they did not want to spend more money on the visa renewal. They told me that for a few weeks they frequented bars away from the city centre and sometimes even other cities within England to meet British women, since there were too many foreigners in the bars and clubs of central London. Their purpose was to meet a British woman who would fall in love with them. Then, they would tell them that they needed to leave the country due to their lack of a visa. In order not to "lose their loved one" they would marry them, allowing them to remain in the country legally. If the marriage did not work out, they could get a divorce after five years, the period required for obtaining permanent residence. According to one of them, some friends had already achieved such a feat, and were already dating English girls.

Besides these cases, there are situations in which migrants purchase a marriage from someone with European citizenship. There are also some instances where the "transaction" is carried out between friends. In such cases, most of the time, the person who has an interest in obtaining citizenship pays for the marriage. Yet this works as a "token" payment. This tactic was used by Aline who married Mario as he had Portuguese documentation. Being friends she only paid him a minimal sum.

A similar case happened to an acquaintance at S. Cleaner, who to obtain the documentation "married" an Italian, his roommate. According to him, it would not be a problem to simulate a gay couple, as they had shared a bedroom for a long time and had many photos of the two of them together.

In the cases in which a marriage is actually purchased, prices range between £2,000.00 and £5,000.00. The main problem is that the "buyer" is bound and dependent on a "stranger" for five years. It was common to hear stories of people who "purchased a marriage" who, after a while, needed to continue giving money to their "partner". Otherwise, the other person only had to ask for a divorce before five years resulting in the marriage being void. In spite of the risk of having to be dependent on a stranger for a few years, many undocumented migrants who didn't wish to leave the country used this tactic, because the fear of being reported or discovered would be worse for them.

In London, stories told by Brazilians about someone who was denounced and deported due to lack of documentation or for working more than the twenty weekly hours allowed to students were circulating. During my time in London, there were very few people who didn't work more than the twenty hours.

> When you coexist too much with Brazilians you hear a lot of histories, about a house that police raided and took ten people, some work area that police raided and took twenty people. You hear this sort of thing a lot among Brazilians. Even people you get to interact with, get to know, were deported; it makes you afraid [Guilherme].

Hatred, envy and greed were always the causes of such denunciations, which created a fear of "staying too much on the scene." That is, migrants always feel obliged to maintain the confidentiality of their situation, even those who had visas. Being "illegal" is not something that marks the subject at all times, and only the fact of working more than twenty hours can turn a legal migrant into "an illegal". The latter situation occurred inside the second house that I lived in. There were nine residents, and amongst them were three Brazilians, one of whom, Julia, was a friend who had gone to London with my help.

Julia arrived in London just before I returned to Brazil. She had a student visa and was working in a pub. Like everyone there, she worked more than the twenty hours allowed, something that everyone in the house had always known. One day Julia began to argue with one resident at her house, an Australian girl. She had the double bed in the girl's bedroom, which they shared. At that time the Australian girl had got a new boyfriend and said that she wanted the double bed. Julia told her that she had been in the house longer than her and would not give her the bed. The Australian, knowing that Julia had a student visa and was working more than the hours allowed, picked up the phone and threatened to call immigration and report her. Afraid of being found out, Julia packed her suitcases that same day and was forced to find another place to live.

Everyone was very fond of Julia, but denunciation was something that precluded any action from the others against the Australian girl. One day, two of the residents discovered that the Australian's Brazilian boyfriend was in the country illegally. They then used the same threat to evict the couple, so that Julia could return.

These situations of denunciations correspond to what Ribeiro (1998) called the "culture of illegals", a phenomenon that permeates extensively the lives of migrants. Due to not knowing the laws of the host country, migrants are exploited because of their fear. As is well known, that "culture" always rests in the denunciation mechanism that would work as a 'panopticon', because anyone can anonymously report someone else at any time. Torresan (1994) compares the fear of being reported amongst Brazilians in London to the type of social control exercised by witchcraft, the belief in an invisible evil that cannot be verified. Therefore, the fear of denunciation is also an instrument of control that regulates the accumulation of goods and prestige. Someone's social and financial development, which until then was seen on "equal" terms, could well become regarded as a source of hatred, envy and greed. Torresan (*idem*) also states that this culture of illegals would be responsible for creating the "disciplined" worker that accepts any task, given its power to make them structurally subordinate and dependent.

Indeed, the fear of denunciation makes the undocumented worker docile. Yet, what appears to happen in practice is that rather than functioning as a 'panopticon', the denunciation based on the culture of illegals fits in more with the way control is developed socially, according to Deleuze (1992) and similarly, perhaps, to the idea of surveillance in Foucault's disciplinary society - as postulated by Ribeiro (1998). For Deleuze, the old disciplines operating in a closed system give way to those of open spaces and without duration, by means of flexible forms of control and not just in certain specific areas. In the case of migrant workers, this control starts already in their passage through Immigration Control at the airport and the fear of being reported makes them feel controlled in all spheres of their life. Even inside their homes, they feel the weight of control. Max repeatedly said that Guilherme and his cousin did not answer the door for fear of the police.

In addition, there is also the "functionality" of these illegalities in cases of the "undocumented migrant". Ribeiro (1998). In San Francisco, USA, for example, a diversity of interests may be noted around the 'illegal', ranging from lawyers and migrant protection agencies to support associations for this group. Eventually, the formation of an illegal and criminal market of foreigners emerges who sell the necessary documentation. At the same time, this type of migrant is functional for the United States economy, due to the large source of cheap labour they represent, mirroring in this sense the case of London. Thus, the possibility of an undocumented migrant living in London is as great now as in previously recorded cases. This is because of the existence of a form of "management" regarding these illegals, which provides gains to individuals dealing with this market: an arrangement which, arguably, even benefits the British economy by supplying cheap labour and therefore reducing business costs.

Telles (2009, 2010), when studying the relation between the informal, illegal and illicit, expressed the well-established notion of the "bazaar economy"! In Brazil, these informal markets may be seen from the perspective of a displacement of this "management of illegalisms" - using the idea of Foucault (1996) when he leaves the legal-illegal binary discussion behind, in order to analyse how laws operate, without any intention of preventing or curbing 'illegalisms'. Indeed, the objective seems to be to differentiate them internally. For Foucault (*idem*) law is a management of 'illegalisms', by the ruling class as a veritable privilege for itself – through allowing services to be undertaken on their behalf by a disempowered, mobile minority. Thus, the law forbids, isolates and takes over the management of illegals not only as physical objects but also as a means by which domination may be exerted over subordinate social orders. Therefore, informal markets, as mentioned by Telles, are functional to the Brazilian economy and as such are "managed" instead of ended. Unsurprisingly, the same happens with migrant workers in developed countries who, due to their functionality for the local economy, are often in transit betwixt an informal, illegal and illicit "status".

3.3 Body and work: feeling the weight of enchantment

As time goes by, the intense life that migrants lead initially, working long hours, going to parties and then working again without resting, begins to decrease. Their bodies cannot take so much effort any longer; the recently arrived migrant loses then that initial devotion that they usually demonstrate at work. The migrant also realizes that it is possible to keep the lifestyle they want without having to work so much. I understood this when I lost five kilos and became very ill.

This kind of intense life also left marks on Rose's body, which caused her to cut down her working hours and parties. She started to go out less, spending her money on travel and theatre tickets, without having the addictive desire to work more than forty hours a week.

> I became very sick. I was very ill. My body has changed so much here in London! Don't talk about my body or I'll become depressed. I'll get a knife and cut myself all up. I'm fat, full of cellulite, varicose veins have burst everywhere; I have purple legs. Damn it, I feel pains in my back... My hands are all dry and peeling because of the products that we use to polish the cutlery. Yeah... that's pretty crazy, when I arrived here I was all pretty, always putting mascara on. I've never been into too much makeup, however mascara, pencil, and a gloss... I have always used a gloss. But over time, Dude, you have no desire to do that here; it is amazing, you don't have the desire to take too much care of your appearance. I think it's the kind of work you do and with the weather and all, it is like: "Oh, I'm going to work and that is it." And you're working like crazy and going out too much and eventually, it stuffs you and your body up [Rose].

Aline equally decreased her work pace and party lifestyle. She began to live as a couple with Caroline, in a steady job with fixed hours in the DS. The salary she received was spent on dinners, theatre, cinema and some travel. For Aline, the enchantment of London lasted only for the first year, when she was a newcomer.

> When I went to live with Caroline, I was already more settled with my life, so I knew that I needed a steady job. I wanted a steady job because I was already in a relationship. You want to travel, want to do your stuff, and my initial phase of partying had finished. In the beginning here you have lots of enthusiasm, I think it is because of freedom. Sexual and musical freedom... It is also a fact that people accept you more for the way you are. It is not the same in Brazil where you have to get dressed from head to toe to go out, as I used to do. Here sometimes I went out wearing trainers, I went to a nightclub and that was it; I enjoyed it. There is great freedom towards drugs too. Here I tried all the drugs I had never experienced in Brazil; I had only experienced marijuana in Brazil. Then it becomes more like a life experience. And the forbidden things; things taste better when you're doing something you've never done before and that is forbidden. Desire, do you know? But over time it passes. I think a year is the time for you to have these illusions: "Hey it is great here! I want to work, I want to do everything" [Aline].

Like Rose, Aline also felt the consequences of the life she led on her body; besides the pain, she also missed being desired and the will to dress up to go out. She even missed being especially careful regarding the things that London "took off" her.

> I miss taking care of myself, I feel bad. And I say to Caroline: "Gee, my nails, my hair, they're fucked, you know?" You don't take as much care with your body because your body is no longer on display all the time. My body has changed so much here, I feel so much pain that I didn't have before. My legs ache here, my back and my feet ache too, just imagine! These are things that I've never had. In Rio I worked in high heels every day, I didn't stand the whole time, but I stood for two hours. Sometimes I worked a dou-

> ble shift on Saturdays, from 9:30 in the morning until 10:30 at night, in high heels, and I didn't get dead tired as I do here with an eight hours shift. It was different; here the work is heavy. I don't know if this is happening also because of my age, I was younger: now I'm older too [Aline].

Max, Priscila and Bernardo also substantially reduced their working hours. Priscila started to work only forty hours a week in the DS and, as she never liked going out too much, she continued spending her money on the processes of visa renewal and some beauty products. Max also cut down his working hours when he became supervisor in the DS, working forty hours per week, with an employment contract. So did Bernardo, who kept working only in the stadium during some days of the week, spending his wages on electronic goods. Everyone said that their bodies couldn't take the kind of life they led at the beginning any longer.

Guilherme also was aware that the type of work he performed initially to keep his lifestyle had a price, and he was already feeling the impact of weariness on his body. He believed that people in London get enchanted with the lifestyle and that they begin to work very hard in order to capitalise on their new circumstances. But there comes a moment when this wears off and everyone starts to slow down because they are exposed to great physical fatigue.

> The matter here is the following: London gives you something but takes away another. London gives you the right to live the life that you want even by cleaning other people's crap, but it takes away your health, Man. I know that in ten years I'll not have the same health I have today; I no longer have the same health I had when I arrived. And if you are not healthy here, if your body is no good, you have nothing because you won't be able to get up early and come back at night. Nobody is made out of iron. And those who come here aiming to save money have to sacrifice themselves... In fact, everyone does sacrifice, especially at first, but afterwards you cannot take it, especially if you have no family. Now, someone who has a family sacrifices themselves for a while and then goes away because you cannot stay forever. I met some people who did it but they were those who had a family, you know? So, it is due

Willesden Junction is a district in North London, which is known nowadays as being a predominately Brazilian area.

to this rush that guys end up taking a "Red Bull" (cocaine), because in the beginning you're craving for work and more work... One of those days I was in a Brazilian restaurant and heard the guys talking, complaining that they work only eight hours a day and they wanted more hours, wanted to do twenty hours in the day. You realize that's a guy who has arrived here recently, because the newcomers are always rushing, especially the poor ones who come here leaving debts in Brazil and have to pay the guys there, and there is still the fear of the police catching you at any time and you would have to go back to Brazil owing money to everyone. Today, I would have to be paid lots of money to do a double shift, because it's not worth it, ah no, at first I'd do it without stopping

> to think, not today, You can have a good life here without working too much [Guilherme].

The pictures presented in this chapter highlights some interesting issues that deserve to be taken up by way of reflection. Curiously, that said, at no point did I stop to think about the reason why I was working so many hours myself. I only started to muse about it when I was no longer in London. After all, a job that is called temporary makes one feel it is unimportant because you can lose it at any time. Conversely, in a number of cases, it actually becomes more valuable than a full-time job, not in the sense that one would have an employment contract which provides one some social security and long-term planning, but rather in the sense of the time worked. This is because you work much longer hours than a legal worker with "regularized" work - most often without a day off or a public holiday and without health insurance. In the case of sickness, neither does the worker receive any type of aid, nor does he or she receive money for the working days they lose, since they only earn money for the hours actually worked.

Therefore, workers earn money through the use of their healthy bodies for a certain period, and if the body is no longer able to work, they have no way to generate income. The person here is nothing but a pure object, a commodity that sells their own body for unspecified lengths of time. The worker doesn't only barter it as a physical force, but sells their appearance and emotions, especially in the service sector where people spend energy,and even incur a financial burden to maintain the employability of their bodies.

An extreme example of the use of the body as a commodity is when the young workers in S. Cleaner served as "guinea pigs" for the pharmaceutical industries. It is well known, of course, that pharmaceutical companies were often testing new drugs and looking for people to be "guinea pigs". The risk of such an experiment would be assumed by the individual who applied to take part in these tests. After all, this service is well remunerated, a fact known to these participants. Moreover, the price varies according to the type of drug being used and the time the person should be under observation. Generally, if it is a drug that in the eyes of the company would not incur many risks, and the "guinea pig" would have to stay about a week in the hotel taking injections and medicines, the payment was around £1500.00. When the company assessed the risk as greater, it paid more. For example, the person would be paid about £10,000.00 to have a portion of the finger cut and sewn back again, in order to evaluate the positive prognosis of the drugs used in the healing process and the body's "acceptance" of the grafted piece.

Many workers at S. Cleaner from the "C Stadium" had earned money at least once with pharmaceutical companies. The people passed information on by "word of mouth" and those who often went through the tests alerted others about the next. According to them, it was a simple job and a good life: the "guinea pig" stays in a hotel playing video games, eating healthy food and even earning a very high amount of cash. It would be the kind of life that some workers had already experienced in Brazil, but it was a rare thing in London. However, as noted in some cases, the person sometimes was not paid enough for the risks undertaken.

One such case refers to a young Brazilian man whose nickname in the company was "Guinea Pig", precisely for providing this type of service on more than one occasion. "Guinea Pig" became aware of a new trial, he turned up on the day scheduled and had taken all previous examinations required. Upon completion of the examinations, he was warned that it could affect the functionality of his kidneys. He received £5,000.00 to spend two weeks in a clinic being given medication for the test. According to what he said, his kidneys stopped working for a certain period.

The most interesting thing to note is that, over time, many end up as if they were embedded in that lifestyle. Even Diego, inserted into the logic of this type of sensibility, came to me one day, proposing that we both do one of these tests in order to earn money fast, without effort. At that moment I even considered the possibility, but ultimately we didn't pursue it.

As demonstrated by Wolkowitz and Warhurst (2010), work is increasingly "embodied". This was intensified especially with the changes in the work process, which resulted in an increasing commodification of bodies, specifically with the increase of working in the service sector. This situation reconfigured the body/mind dualism, putting an end to the separation of "bodily" and "intellectual" activity.

Workers are not only selling part of their bodies, they are equally selling their emotions, appearance and strength. No wonder that while I was working in the DS the company paid for three 'customer service' courses for waiters, including myself, to learn how to control our feelings and provide the customer with a "celebrity" stay. The customer, according to these courses, should be treated like anyone famous who would receive this "happy service", even if they mistreated us. In some situations, the managers had to choose the "better looking" waiters to carry out some important events. This demand came from people who hired DS to hold events.

Although there is this demand in the labour market, and workers often need to undergo long working hours without complaining to avoid losing their jobs, the issue of "work to maintain the lifestyle" can't be brushed aside.

Even for me, as I have already mentioned, I needed at a certain time to work over seventy hours a week, which made me sick, not being able to sleep or eat properly. Even though at this time there was no longer the necessity to carry out as much work – I was already established in the company and I earned enough to cover my expenses every month– I wanted to work the maximum hours possible. Besides wanting to earn money to travel and spend on holidays through the various shifts that I started doing, there was a matter of prestige both inside and outside the job, since in the house, those who worked more were held in more respect by other residents. This similarly happened within the company, amongst workers. As already noted earlier, the more shifts a week the worker had, the more prestige among co-workers, for it was a sign that the company was valuing the worker[29].

Nevertheless, as demonstrated in all the cases presented here, as time passes, the excitement of working and the energy of spending eighty hours a week at it decreases, mainly because the body stops responding.

29 A similar situation was also verified by Sales (1999b) among Brazilians in Boston, as well as in London. In general it is very common for newcomers to enter this logic of working hard and for long hours, which ultimately results in a competition among these workers to see who worked more during the week, because working hard means prestige. As in London, in Boston it is common to hear the conversations of newcomers staff saying proudly that he "did" ninety hours, a hundred hours of work in a week.

In addition, when this initial enchantment finishes, these individuals realize that even when working less, they manage to maintain a lifestyle still seen by some as better than what they had in Brazil, either to continue consuming or have a “freer” life in London.

It is interesting to observe that the issue of ease of consumption, one way or another, remains present in most statements, even the statements of those who have already slowed down, not working as much as before. This is especially the case with those who redefine their initial plans to spend two or three years in London, who work and accumulate money to stay in the city for a longer period, given the ease of consumption.

CHAPTER 4

BRAZILIAN SOCIABILITY: STATUS, CONFLICT AND PREJUDICE

4.1 Migrant as a winner

The issue of consumption becomes relevant in several trajectories. However, it is noteworthy how the goods consumed carry, often, the symbolic brand of the "winner", both for the group with which migrants live in the receiving society, in this case the Brazilians in London, and for those who they left in Brazil, principally through social networks like Facebook and Orkut.

I remember when I was first flying to London with Diego, he said:

> Do you know what I'm afraid of, Man? I'm afraid of not returning with that sense of accomplishment, you know? Or that I'll have to return before the time we could support us here, or return without learning English. That scares me [Diego].

When Diego said that, I realized that I shared the same fears—a fear of failing to win that challenge that we had proposed to face: live in another country, support ourselves on our own and learn a new language. Moreover, at the beginning when I was still without work, feeling alone, suffering the cold and seeing the little money I had finishing, I used to call home and when talking to my parents, I never complained, cried or anything like that. When I hung up the phone, I would cry, but never when I was talking to them. Of course I didn't want to worry them and could not admit that things were not going right or that I was being a "loser".

Many people said the same thing when we engaged in this kind of conversation about family and friends in Brazil. Rose, as noted earlier, had told me that she hid from all her friends when she was deported on her first visit to London. She only tried to return to England so that she wouldn't have to meet her friends and say that she had been unable to enter the country. Aline also said she suffered a lot in the beginning, but she never spoke of that to her parents and friends in Brazil.

> At first I cried a lot, I cried, I cried... but I didn't tell them... I wouldn't pass it on to my parents. I never cried on the phone with them, never, not at all [Aline].

When someone migrates, the person is migrating to win, to improve their lives, whether for economic, cultural, private or family matters. The person moves to build a better life and therefore needs to keep that image for those who stayed behind: the consumption of goods and travel often serving to justify their position socially in a context where the most diverse forms of unqualified labour are carried out, types of work they would hardly ever have performed in Brazil.

I remember that Diego and José at the same time, when they were travelling across Europe, posted photos on their Facebook profiles to show the people in Brazil that they were visiting new places. Diego would also post photos working at the stadium; although he was working as a cleaner, the photos showed him watching the matches of the Champions League in Europe, something that all his friends would like to do in Brazil. I did the same, and on each photo I posted, people would comment about the good life we were leading in Europe. It is clear that they did not know that we spent the whole morning cleaning bathrooms, picking up rubbish, suffering from the cold and sometimes even going hungry.

As for those a little older, who worked and had a more stable life in Brazil, it would not look well to say we were cleaners in London, as in the case of Rose. When I asked her about the work she performed in London and what her friends would say if they saw her doing that, she replied:

> I don't mind doing these jobs because I don't know anyone here. So I know that nobody is going to see me and say: "Damn it, look at Rose, how depressing, working as a waitress." If it was in Rio, I would never do it. I never tell that I take care of a bathroom, or that I have worked as a cleaner; I have never told anyone. I say that I'm working in a bar, in a restaurant. "What do you do?" "Oh, I'm a runner". They don't know what a "runner" is. It sounds classy. So I'm not putting a lot of pictures on my Facebook. I posted photos of a few trips, a festival that I went to and some photos with the girls in the snow, that is all. Now once a motherfucker put a picture of me when I was wearing a tie and a black shirt (waitress uniform). I said, "Take it off now, don't ever do it again in your life" [Rose].

Priscila equally says that performing this type of underemployment in London does not bother her, first, because it does not seem to be her life, as she doesn't even have any Brazilian friends living with her. Second, a waitress in England still appears, in Brazil's local eyes, to have better standing than the same job at home. Indeed, for Priscila Londoners see jobs differently from Brazilians. As she recalled, the daughter of the president of the DS worked part-time as a waitress at the company in which her father was the president, often serving her own father and friends. In addition, the social circle of which she was part of, were composed of people who were all doing the same sort of job. Yet, like Rose, she herself did not reveal to people in Brazil the kind of life she led in London.

The comments that "people don't know what we do in London" - and "when we speak the name in English it is chic" - as Rose said, always emerged in rounds of conversation. Once Max commented about Maria, a woman about 35 years old from São Paulo, who worked with him cleaning offices, that one day they were working together and Maria's mother telephoned her. She couldn't talk because she was at work. To solve this sudden issue, she answered the call and said she'd phone back later because Mr. Hoover was coming soon. Max asked who Mr. Hoover was, only to be told that she could not tell her mother that she worked as a cleaner. Instead, she had said that she was working in an office as a secretary and her boss was Mr. Hoover (vacuum cleaner). Thus, she would never forget the name of her boss.

Max told a similar story about visiting a racetrack with a friend from Capão Redondo a few months previous. For £1000.00 you could go for a drive on the racing circuit. As his friend Juliano loved racing, he paid £1000.00 and went for a drive. Max's friend took pictures with overalls and driving the vehicle. When he was on holiday in Capão Redondo, people asked him how life in London was and questioned him about the people. One of them then said: "Gee, Juliano is doing well for himself." Max, not understanding, because Julian was a kitchen porter in London, asked in what way? His friend replied:

> Don't you know it? He became a test pilot of a racing team, I spoke to him on the internet a few days ago and he told me. I didn't believe it, ah no, but have a look on his Facebook [Max, repeating his friend's comment].

That day, Max made a point of looking up his friend on Facebook to show him the photos he had taken. Max likewise assessed Bernardo's homepage on the same network. At that time, Bernardo was out of work; his cousin had to pay his rent and he owed money to people since he had bought a motorcycle, which he had already sold. Bernardo had just posted on his Facebook's homepage a photo of a motorcycle and a car, saying they were his 'passions', also posting a picture of a luxury van saying that he would buy the van in a few months' time. After hearing this, I started to look at some of the pages on Facebook of people I knew and history repeated itself. People were always posting messages and photos on the site to keep up this idea that they were winners in London.

Thus cars, travelling and buying goods function as objects of status for those who were cleaning toilets and serving people, as Max said. Dating a foreigner also serves as a form of distinction, both for people who are in Brazil and for Brazilians living in London. Proof of this came from comments I heard from a Brazilian who worked at S. Cleaner, who used to come to my house with Diego. They always made jokes such as: "Junior is doing well in London: he is a waiter serving doctors, and even has an Australian girlfriend". Max, however, had a more critical view saying that the vast majority of girls in London just wanted to interact with foreigners to get a passport and increase their status among Brazilians.

> Most people around here do that (they get married for the document). And also to go to Brazil, like that girl who worked with us there, she took her boyfriend to Brazil saying: "Oh, my boyfriend is *gringo*!" "My boyfriend is handsome, wonderful and *gringo*. He doesn't speak Portuguese, he is white and he has good hair." She started to speak in front of all her friends, speaking English with the guy. This is what status means to her. What she really wanted was to show the guy off. Orkut, Facebook and stuff like that Dude, they serve to show that people are well, the guys show off, they put two hundred photos a day on Facebook, because they want to show that they are well, to show to family and friends that they are dating a "*gringo*" or a "*gringa*" or that they're buying the whole world and living like a playboy. Which are all lies, because the guy is here (Bernardo), just because he is on a motorcycle he gets a big head, he doesn't have a penny and is living on money borrowed from others, when he gets paid his wages, he pays the loan, when he runs out of money in the middle of month he borrows more. You will see, if you take your girlfriend to Brazil, you will become a celebrity among your friends [Max].

In addition to this attempt to maintain status for those in Brazil, the same must also be maintained between the Brazilians who are in London. There was always talking about who had bought the newest clothing, computers, bikes and cars. When going to a party with Brazilians it was a common thing that people bought drinks. There was always someone who stood up and said that he would pay for a round of beer for everyone. The first Brazilian party that I went to was with Max. He had warned me not to buy drinks, because there was always someone wanting to demonstrate a better life than the others, and they would spend the night buying drinks. That was something people did (it was the reason why Max always said that he did not want to get involved with Brazilians in London).

> You go to a Brazilian nightclub here, there is one that has a huge silver chain; there is another that has a huge gold chain. What for? The guy at the nightclub on the weekend, he is a celebrity. From Monday to Friday he is a cleaner, cleaning other people's crap in the bathroom. So, he gets shit all over his hands from Monday to Friday and on weekends he puts a silver chain around his neck and he thinks he is Silvio Santos[30]. So, as you asked me once if the Brazilians change when they come here, the answer is yes, they do, because they think that just because they are here they are celebrities, they are starlets. They are not normal citizens [Max].

Max's last comment illustrates several things that I heard during my time here: "Brazilians change when they are in London, they always want to look richer than the others, to show that they are good. Thus, they play tricks on everyone, they are not trustworthy."

4.2 Brazilians as seen by Brazilians: Conflict and distinction.

As one may observe, there are different "types" of Brazilians doing so-called unqualified jobs in London. They are living this "difference" all the time. Hence, most of these migrants do not look favourably upon their countrymen, which results in an "intra-community division."

Guilherme realized that there was such a division between Brazilians and, for Guilherme, this happened according to the "status" of each migrant. In other words, he saw they would be defined by the possession or not of documentation. As this demonstrates, there is more a discourse of a conflict situation rather than one of solidarity.

30 Silvio Santos: a famous personality in Brazil who has his own TV Show every Sunday.

> Dude, there are many sorts of Brazilians here. There is the student, the illegal and the legal migrants. There are three sorts of Brazilians here and one doesn't bump into another, they don't have contact with each other. The student is the guy who comes here with the visa and doesn't come with concerns about saving money. The guy takes weekends off, going to the Netherlands, Italy and France. These folks have a social life and an interest in knowing the local and regional culture as well. They are people who engage even with foreigners; they have more foreign friends. They leave here and go to Australia to spend a vacation, their friends go to Brazil, and they can afford to keep going back and forth. Their lifestyles are different from that of migrants; they don't come here to see the underworld such as illegals do. Students have a social life; they go to nightclubs and such. As to illegals, especially at first, they are afraid to go out, try to save money and such. The guy who is here legally is also different because he doesn't keep spending money on documents, visa and so on; many of them are even small business men. [Guilherme]

Guilherme's perception, attached to the issue of the visa, was linked to his experience as an undocumented migrant, which was contrasted with the similar situation experienced by Max, a resident in the same house and holder of a European passport. In certain circumstances, the conversations at their house involved the discussion of Brazilians in London. Max always made critical and negative comments in relation to Brazilians.

A few days before having this conversation with Guilherme, I witnessed one of these discussions. We were eating pizza in Max's bedroom. Guilherme and Bernardo were also present. Max started to tell us that he had seen on television a robbery that occurred in a jewellery store in central London and the cameras had recorded some images. He said that "the guys" were on motorcycles and wearing black helmets. Two of them stopped the traffic and two others went with the bikes on the sidewalk of the store. They broke the glass display case, grabbed the jewellery and fled. After explaining the scene, Max added that he was sure they were Brazilians: first, because English people don't know that kind of trickery, secondly, by way they were driving the motorbikes. They could only be Brazilians.

At the time everyone agreed and said they also believed the thieves were Brazilians, even though this was only based on Max's story. This kind of talk was repeated several times, "had to be a Brazilian " or "could only be a Brazilian". For Guilherme, this discourse was made by those who were holders of legal documentation, making reference to undocumented Brazilians.

> There is a strong prejudice around here. Do you know, a prejudice from Brazilians towards Brazilians? For example, you have your visa, your European passport, then a guy comes along doing something that you don't think it's cool, anything, and you say: "He is Brazilian." "Ah, I don't know what: he is Brazilian." "There was a fight? It is Brazilian." There is a Brazilian guy saying this all the time, like: "That's why I don't go to that place, because there are Brazilians and blah, blah, blah." Then, the ones who are here legally, they think the illegals ones are wrong for being here. The Brazilians themselves think they are above the others just because of a piece of paper (visa). But I have a fucking life in Brazil, now why don't I have the right to change my life? Only he has a right, because of a piece of paper? Even the guy who didn't have the document, when he gets the document, that is it, the guy turns into a superman, this is the reality here. [Guilherme]

Guilherme's view is interesting, but somehow it gets a little too rigid regarding the issue of visas determining the lifestyle that people lead. As he says, many of those who go to London, in order to work and make money, end up getting into a situation of illegality. With time, however, they begin to lead a life of partying and nightclubs, as the students do. On the other hand, many students also end up finding themselves in situations of illegality and often work more than those who had migrated with the initial interest in saving money.

There is no denying, however, that the visa issue is a distinguishing factor, not only to facilitate the way these migrants have their experiences in London, but it is also a symbolic issue, since being "illegal" refers to that concept of the economic migrant as poor and inferior. It is no wonder that Priscila was keen to show me all her visas that she had already renewed when people at the DS suspected that she was in the country illegally. This was especially because she was known as either "Paraiba", as Rose called her sometimes, or "conterrania[31]", as Max and his girlfriend referred to her, and all said she was probably, like anyone from the Northeast in Brazil, here illegally. A comment by Rose expressed this connection of the undocumented migrant with the poor Brazilian who migrates to work abroad.

> I've thought about buying a marriage. Everyone thinks that when you're in London, everything here is possible. In London you buy a marriage, buy a man, buy drugs and buy parties. Now, a fake document, never! I am too cowardly to do this, and even more so because of the things I went through (Immigration Control), never. Illegal? No way. I'd rather go back to my country. I'm not starving, I didn't come here to save money, I came here so I wouldn't have to live with my mother, it is very different. [Rose]

This bias becomes so significant that some say they don't reveal their origin anymore in their jobs, because Brazilian migrants are all seen as "ignorant." Yet, sometimes the issue is not the document that creates this stereotype, but regional origin, which connects, for example, the person from Goias (*goiano*) to the poor and uneducated.

> I've always said I was one (a Brazilian), until I started interacting with the Brazilians here. Like this Eliza from the pizzeria, the one from the whipping post (reference to slavery; Rita is black), from Goiás... what a race, what a race! The people from the countryside who come here are fucked up. You and Diego are the only people from the countryside who can really speak decent Portuguese. Like a woman who works with me speaks of her son: "Oh, I want him to *do study* Rose." Fuck, the basic, my sister, speak at least the basic: "I want him to study." "Oh, I want him to *do study*, Rose. I just want it." No, my sister, you can study what you want, if you don't speak your own language you do not speak any language, it is impossible. I cannot understand it, I work with a lot of Brazilians, most of them are from Goiás; I'm not discriminating against them, but the reality is that they are ignorant people. I don't even

31 Paraiba and conterranea are negative ways to call people who call from the North East of the country.

> say they are poor because I'm also poor. But they are ignorant and they come here with the dream of making money, because that's what they want. For them, it is the dream of earning money to purchase a small plot of land, as they say, and build a house. Working with whoever comes here to save money is hell. A bunch of greedy people who want to outsmart each other in order to exploit; it sucks. [Rose]

Like Rose, many express the same opinion about Brazilians in everyday life in London. The idea of "dirty Brazilians" (physically and morally) also appears in several statements, as with Priscila's comment:

> I think the Brazilians here are a filthy race. I think everybody here is after money; that is the impression I get. Everyone's after money, everyone wants to outsmart you. It is not only a few; it is a heap of them, who don't want to do it. If you have two jobs, he wants three, he wants to take your place at your job and he wants to get more hours at work than you. Because it's like I told you, those Brazilians who have something better to do, come here, do what they came here to do and leave. The Brazilians who come here to earn money are from Goias. Wherever you go, you meet a *goiano* [Priscila].

With these lines, one notices that there is the creation, among Brazilians, of "us vs' them", where "them", or the "other" is linked to the image of the economic migrant, that poor human being, without culture, who comes from a poorer place, with the sole purpose of working. While in the U.S. the inferior Brazilian appears with a regional cut-out in the figure of a person from Minas Gerais, here he is materialized in the figure of a person from Goias.

Guilherme believed that this distinction was produced from the issue of the document, a bias from those with documents against those who were undocumented. However, the document is only one of these markers of difference (race, colour, regionalism, gender, class, documentary situation, language - well-spoken Portuguese or English - and others) that intersect at the time of forming this image of an inferior Brazilian. An example of this is when Rose mentions the fact that many of these

Tower of a Catholic Church in Willesden Junction where mass other religious activities are minister by Brazilian priest in Portuguese.

ignorant Brazilians hold visas, but they don't know how to use them. They are allowed to travel, but they only want to work:

> Then I think that Brazilians living in London are a total disappointment. The Brazilians are seen as ignorant or as prostitutes and as bums. Brazilians come here, start as cleaners, earning £5.00 or £6.00 per hour; it is great, they are happy. They work fifteen hours to buy their little plot of land and that is great. They don't

> think about progressing or climbing. "Oh, I want to do that, I want to do the other." They continue in the same place. And there's a lot of them that have a passport, thus they can travel and don't leave here. I don't travel because unfortunately I have to have the fucking visa to go anywhere here, understand? However here, there is a lot of illegals, but there is a lot of people who has a passport, they work full time, live all crammed in the same house and in the same bedroom [Guilherme].

Therefore, as the document is not the determinant, the regional issue alone will not be the sole issue either, because often those who are considered "*Goianos*" are not from Goiás at all, reminiscent, as this is of a statement by Rose, shown earlier, where she was referring to Rita as "*Goiana*". Rita is not from Goias but for Rose she represents the figure of people from Goiás in London, most likely because she is black, didn't speak English very well and had gone to London with the intention of working. The same happened when I asked Priscila who these Brazilians are, who "want to outsmart everybody", and she promptly said that they are those who are in London for money, the "*Goianos*". However, when I asked Priscila whether these people are indeed from Goiás, she ends up getting confused and saying that among the *goianos* she knew there were also people from Paraná, another Brazilian state:

> Those Brazilians who have been here for years are the ones who want to make money, it is the *goiano* who wants to make money, who wants to rob a bank, who wants whatever, who are here for years. *Goianos* overtake London, usually they work in the kitchen, you come into the kitchen and see a lot of them, said Priscila.
> - But where do you interact with so many *Goianos*? - I then asked her.
> - At the store where I worked there was a lot, there were so many *goianos* in the kitchen!- Priscila says.
> - But they were really from Goiás? - I asked her.
> - Well, when I worked there, there was really a *Goiano*, and a lot of people from Paraná... And where was there more *Goianos*?! Ah... Usually they are actually in the kitchen! – Priscila said.

Priscila said the above during a conversation with Rose and myself. Rosa agreed with Priscila: "The *Goianos* took over London, doing the

A drawing of Rio which one of the interviewees doodled in the kitchen.

dirtiest jobs, like the kitchen porters. They just think about money; they speak neither English nor correct Portuguese and take advantage of everyone." Priscila realized they were both making generalizations, so she tried to change a little of the tone of the conversation:

– So you haven't interacted with so many *Goianos*, Priscila!
– Ah, then, I have met three people that are really from Goiás and they belonged to an evangelical church, so they were good

people. It was like that, you saw them and they said they were here to work and make money, but they are good people, you see that they are of good character. They are not like that person who is there to hurt you. Now one thing I'm going to mention and that is when people say: "Oh those illegal people coming here to work." A friend of mine came talking about it and said: "Oh Priscila, these people eat poorly, they don't eat properly." I said: "Look, I have to give Caesar what is Caesar's, these people eat better than I do. I only eat frozen food because I also don't cook. I eat only at work; they eat better than I do. If they do a test here to see how my health is, their health is better than mine." - Priscila argues.
"I agree, because they eat rice, beans, meat every day. But also, they have to eat well... They work fucking hard." Rose tells her.
"But Rose, don't you work hard as well?" I ask.
"Yeah... if you stop to think about it... I work very hard too," she replies.

For Rose, however, it didn't matter how much she worked, sometimes even more than those who theoretically would be in London to just work, she was not an migrant, she was not like them, she was from Rio, she was white, came from a good family, and even if she worked hard, she knew how to enjoy life in London. As I noticed when our conversation continued:

"So, I think what really differentiates one thing from another is when you come from a good family. If you come from a good family, you will be a good person. And most of these Brazilians living in London aren't. They are people, I wouldn't even say humble; they are ignorant people who only think about money. It's what I was telling you, they don't go to the theatre or a museum—this is almost free; there are thousands of museums—and they don't travel! You are in the right place to travel," Rose says.
"It is not like that Rose, I met two girls from Goiás here who were "normal"; good people. Normal," Priscila says, contradicting herself.
"You have to introduce me to them then, because I haven't met any Goiana who was a good person," Rose adds.
"Rose, everyone, everywhere has their exceptions. Everything in

> life has its exception. I met two normal girls, super nice people." Priscila ends.

Most likely Priscila began with this speech that every place has its exception, due to realizing that, besides the fact all those she called *Goianos* were not from Goiás, she was making generalizations and using biased phrases against people from a specific region of Brazil, something that she also felt reflexively when they started talking about the Northeast, since she was from Pernambuco.

Although Priscila is white, has completed high school and has come from a traditional family (factors that are likely to preclude her from seeing herself as a "*Goiana*") occasionally she was referred to by Brazilian people from the south and southeast, as a "conterranea" or "Paraiba", when it was felt necessary by others to speak of her as an inferior. That amounted to saying she a poor migrant who was in London merely to work. In these decisive moments, when small hierarchies were formed, she became included in these other "inferiorized" terms.

In such cases, one can see that within this process of differentiation between Brazilians, at a more "macro" level, there is the creation of the inferior "other", in which prejudice is embodied in the figure of the *Goiano*, representing the poor, dirty, "illegal", uneducated migrant. These "markers" of difference intersect when the image of the *Goiano* is formed.

Yet, even when small scale interaction take place, it is possible to see hierarchies being created and broken at all times. This includes those who are not initially considered "*goianos*", producing markers being activated to rank a relationship on a more micro level. In other words, when necessary, Rose became the "*carioca*" and Priscila the "Paraiba", while Max and Jessica became the "*Paulistanos*" and Priscila the "conterranea". At other times, Max was the "Brazilian" and Rose the "Bolivian" bitch, whereas Rose was the "*Carioca*" from a good family and Max and Jessica were "Paraibas" of São Paulo, who smelt.

A situation that illustrates these hierarchies being negotiated on a micro level of interaction took place when Rose argued with kitchen workers at the pizzeria. At that time she had not yet learned the local language and was often subjected to unpleasant situations. For her, most of her supervisors at work belonged to this group of "scum" and she didn't accept taking orders from a "black" or a "Paraiba" like Rita.

> I'm not going to work in that stinky place any longer, it is full of Brazilian scum; I'm not black to work as a slave, wiping the shit of others. Who does this black woman (Rita) thinks she is to give me orders? They can't even speak Portuguese properly and they want to give me orders?! [Rose].

It was at that moment of breaking the hierarchy that phrases like Priscila's emerged: "In Brazil I was not biased but here I had to become biased because the blacks here think they are people." This type of statement is made at all times by those that in Brazil, theoretically, belong to groups considered dominant, not only in the economic scale, but also in all symbolic spheres that generate distinctions. People who are white, middle class and studied until the third grade did not perform in Brazil the same type of unqualified work they did in London.

This existing conflict and lack of trust among the Brazilians makes the issue of lack of friends and loneliness seem, to some, as one of the main difficulties in continuing to live in London.

CHAPTER 5

NEGOTIATING THE RETURN: FREEDOM, LONELINESS AND PERMANENT PRESENT[32]

Once the initial euphoria with London life had passed, and the pace of work had decreased, some began to negotiate their lives again, thinking about a possible return, but without planning much for the future. Issues such as climate and loneliness seemed possible factors in promoting a return to the homeland.

32 Nardi (2003), when citing some authors (LASCH, 1990; BECK, GIDDENS & LASH, 2000), demonstrates how the economic, political, technological and social changes, which began in the 1970s and intensified in the next two decades, would also have changed the way individuals start to see the world around them. New values began to be created within a new social reality that emerges and a new person also begins to get built in this scenario. These changes were reflected in a contemporary moral code that is linked to the increase of individualism, the weakness of the social bond, the creation of a culture of narcissism, at the prospect of a society of uncertainty, extreme competition and the dismantling of the guarantees of stability, resulting in a situation where individuals no longer work with the possibility of long-term planning and thought directed to the construction of a future. In this new model immediate gratification becomes the objective "of life" and temporality is now marked by the idea of a permanent present, where actions are increasingly focused on the self-realization of the individual and not for the "group" itself, like religion, children, close friends or society as a whole. For Bauman (2001) and Sennett (2006), this instant gratification would be realized today, for many, by way of consumption.

Rose intended to live in Rio de Janeiro again someday, but she was unsure about when or of what she will do, if she returned. She wanted to stay in London for a long time; however, the biggest problem was not having the documentation and the constant need to save money to renew her visa. Indeed, due to not working as hard as she had before, whenever she was required to renew her visa, she needed to stop going out and travelling, in order to save money for this purpose.

Rose wouldn't accept staying in the country illegally, and because she also didn't find anyone she could trust to "do business" with, i.e., someone to "buy" a European marriage, she continued renewing visas without making many plans. She also complained about the climate, since the London winter was very cold and "lifeless" for a woman from Rio, used to the beach and having "lots of fun". Yet, the style of life she had in London, marked by an immediate and easy access to nightlife and travel, still weighed heavily on her mind when asked about returning to Brazil.

> I wanted to stay, but I didn't want to stay as a student. It sucks to be always renewing my visa; I'm already going for the third renewal. I would like to have a document to be able to do what I wanted. If I want to live in Spain tomorrow, I 'm going to Spain, if I want to live in Italy, I will... You know, I wanted to be a gypsy. In Brazil I never lacked anything. My job in a store was quiet, I was all cute, having coffee with my clients, or Coca-Cola, chatting, and while chatting I would sell to them. So it was easy money in a place where I didn't have to do heavy lifting; it wasn't dirty and I became friends with the customers and I went to my client's parties. But here it is easier and faster, and the money is worth more. In Brazil I never lacked anything, but you need to plan things and I never planned my life. But, for example, there, I know that if I wanted to travel it would be more difficult. I want to continue traveling to Europe, the United States, Thailand, because I want to go to Thailand. I'm going to renew my visa and, God willing, I will go... I'm now working for it, to make money... I'm going to renew my visa for two years with this marketing course I've just paid for. I'm going to save money and stay 15 to 20 days in Thailand. It is a thing I know I could never do in Brazil, with a

> saleswoman's salary. When you asked once what makes me get me up in the cold every day here and go to work, I think today I have the desire to save money to continue traveling. I will travel more, I want to go to Thailand, I want to go to Japan, I want to go to New Zealand… I want to be free... [Rose].

In addition to this easiness found in London for "consuming", as well as the free lifestyle she wanted, Rose also pointed out the factors in Brazil that made her want to stay a little longer.

> I'm very afraid of returning to Brazil. Deep inside my heart I have a great desire to return, but I feel afraid when I say that I'm going back to Rio. Afraid of not getting something good over there that would guarantee my freedom as well. Furthermore, there is the matter of violence over there. My mother even told me that I wouldn't get used to living in Rio again, and I think that's true. Here I ride the bus alone the whole night with money in my handbag and all, and I don't care because I know nothing is going to happen. And there's the issue of family problems. If I'm in Rio, the family problem is with me. Aline is always asking me: "Rose, why you don't want to go back to Brazil?" The reason is because I've got nothing to hold me here and if I want to go back to Brazil tomorrow, I'll go back. I have no boyfriend, I have no husband, I don't have a great job, I have absolutely nothing [Rose].

This may be the reason why Rose wished to stay longer; precisely for the very things that she "doesn't have" in London: "responsibilities", such as a husband and a regular job that would make her take root and limit the free and flexible life that she had grown accustomed to. Clearly she was aware that she has already worked hard and carried out "dirty" work that she would never do in Brazil to maintain the lifestyle she wanted. Rose commented that she hated the kind of work that she performed. She would have preferred to work in a shop selling clothes; however, as long as none of her friends from Rio de Janeiro saw her working as a waitress or cleaner, she didn't mind. Therefore, the type of work she performed was no longer central and didn't give meaning to her existence. It was only a means of access to the "free" lifestyle that pleased her so much.

A very similar situation was found in Priscila's trajectory. Priscila - who had now been in London for five years - while saying she was starting to warm to the idea of returning to Brazil, wasn't sure when she would return. She was tired of doing hard work and she had become disenchanted with life in London a long time prior to this. She was not going out anymore, she was always spending her money on the visa renewal processes and she still had to serve people and put up with annoying managers. She also felt very lonely, people were always coming and going, while she remained in this foreign city. However, she did not know what would become of her life, because, at the same time as she felt tired, she had just paid £2000.00 to a lawyer for ensuring she could stay in London for five more years.

The reason for all this indecision over her return was the same reason she had for coming to London: the relationship with her mother and grandmother. Despite believing that she was now more mature and could now face both of them, the fact that she never saved any money in all these years in London would place her again in a position of dependence on her mother.

> I haven't saved money, I've never even tried it, nor do I have enough work to do that, as I used to do at the beginning. Rose asked me about going back, I told her was that if I go back to Brazil now I don't even have a penny to rent an apartment if I want. But let's see, I wanted to stay until the end of the year to sort things out in my head about returning, because I'll have to face my mother and my grandmother [Priscila].

Thus, she was still negotiating about a possible return, while at the same time she continued to lead an migrants life, doing work that, as she says, a person well raised would not perform in Brazil. Yet, by serving people in London, she could lead her life the way she wanted.

Bernardo and Guilherme were also beginning to warm to the idea of return;

> When I came here I never thought I would spend seven years living here. I miss the people over there (Brazil), I'm here for seven

> and a half years alone, but, you see, the lifestyle of everyone there is different. Whereas here I buy everything I would never buy there, even working less than I did before [Bernardo].

In the last conversation I had with Bernardo in early 2011, he said he would return to Brazil at the end of the year; however, after the holiday season, he would return to London, although he still didn't know if he would try to get a tourist visa again or if he would buy a "hot" passport from people that made Italian passports in Brazil. As for Guilherme, he planned to stay longer until he got something in Brazil that would guarantee stability when he returned.

> My intention now is to go to Italy, get a passport, go back and work less. Staying there legally will enable me to do an English course that also will open more doors for me here. My intention now is to spend ten years here, actually I don't know how long yet, I extended my time here because it is useless to spend too much time planning. I already gave that up. I now have a bill in Brazil... I have paid a deposit for an apartment of the *Minha Casa Minha Vida* Program[33]. I'm going to pay the instalments there and all the rest is really in London. Because I don't know how long I'm going to stay here for. So I want to learn English, to get out of here with something more, and see if I can pay for a couple of apartments, because if one day I get fed up of this here I'll have to leave [Guilherme].

Thus, Guilherme carried on keeping the idea of return in his mind, thereby creating some alternatives in case he returned to Brazil, like buying two apartments and learning English. However, he was afraid of going back and having difficulty readjusting, as had happened with many Brazilians he met in London.

> Because a lot of people say that people who stay here for a long time don't readjust in Brazil when they go back, and this frightens me. Because you come here, you earn R$ 4,000, R$ 5,000 a month, and there you earned R$ 500.00. You won't go back to earn only R$ 500.00. But I'm not like my cousin (Bernardo) who leads

---

33 A Brazilian federal government program that promotes social housing through financial incentives

> a normal life here, spending all the money he has and still owing money to everyone, because I can become fed up with all this and go away. The cold weather and the loneliness here are fucked, man. Loneliness has also decreased slightly, because before, when I spoke no English, it was much worse. You don't understand what people are saying; it's complicated, you feel tired and excluded. So I don't know, Man, I'm living here, but trying to improve my life here, in case I go back to Brazil, so I have a place to live and I can speak English [Guilherme].

It is due to loneliness, that, despite having no plans to return anytime soon, Guilherme carried on trying to buy these "capital investments", the apartment and English language skills, as alternatives for his life upon returning to Brazil someday.

In spite of being "married" to Caroline, loneliness was the reasons for Aline that made her to want to return to Brazil. The safe and calm life that Aline had since becoming a supervisor in the DS seemed to no longer satisfy her, and she felt like something was lacking.

As she was now more mature and well established, even sexually, she began to contemplate her return. However, Caroline, who is now the manager of a unit in the pizzeria where she worked, had no intention of returning. Whereas Aline even sent some resumes to sales companies in Rio de Janeiro. She was called to interviews for two of them, but ended up not going. Thus, she kept the possibility of returning at any time as an option, and meanwhile she has just moved into an apartment to live alone with Caroline, buying furniture and objects that speak more about settling down than returning.

In fact, Aline led her life without planning anything in the long term. One day she was happy, paying for courses and buying goods and services: indications of a greater permanence. Then on some other day, especially in winter, she would wake up wanting to throw away everything and go back for good.

> Maybe my life has fallen into boredom again, and if I go to Brazil it might again fall into boredom over there. For me things are

> moved by this, this desire... relationships, new emotions, do you understand? And they are short and immediate things. Do you want to see? I was thinking about it today. I think that, definitely, I won't have children, neither she nor I, and yeah, if we decide to stay here another year or two, we'll take the money we're saving and we're going to travel; this is our plan. Let's go travelling, let's enjoy it. Because, yeah, to make money, to buy an apartment, and... What for? Let's live now, we're young, we can enjoy traveling. And when we go back to Brazil, we'll have knowledge, we'll have life experience and professional experience too. She is the manager of a restaurant. Besides, she is a chemist in Brazil, she speaks English. I think we have several options to consider carefully. From there, yes, we settle down, get a job and rent an apartment [Aline].

Perhaps the fact of being in a steady relationship and having a secure job, always going through the same routine every day, made Aline miss what she had grown accustomed to in London: a flexible and freer life. Because, as she says, after she began dating Caroline, her life was restricted to working and dating. Hence, she had scarcely any more friends in London and had no social life apart from her girlfriend's circle of acquaintances, or the people that she worked with. She seemed to live in a pendulous dilemma of "freedom vs' security." When she reached the apex of freedom, she missed a safe life: when she achieved a safe life, she missed her freedom.

> I was too much like: "It has to be now", it has to be done yesterday, and that thing too, do you know? The need of sex; I've always felt these things, very strongly. There was certain nights that I went out and said to myself: "Today I have to be with someone, I need to get laid, because if I don't I won't be able to sleep." Today I have calmed down, but sometimes I miss it too, and my social circle here is very reduced [Aline].

In the midst of all this indecision, whether to stay or return to Brazil, Aline thought that life in London, in addition to being a learning experience for life as a whole, was equally best seen as professional development. If, therefore, she returned one day to Brazil, she would have evolved. Indeed, the DS paid for several management and administrative courses and her English was now very good. Furthermore, she could add to her resume a supervisor's position in an international company, which would be "capital" if she returned to Brazil. In addition, besides all the issues already mentioned, she still saw the privilege inherent in staying in London, despite being far from friends and family, not to mention the cold, which she considered the worst part of living in Europe.

> Well, here you're in a developed country. You're in a first world country. There is the safety issue here, and it weighs. You have the issue of transport, transport facilities, consumption facilities. Your purchasing power is greater here. You feel more the power of money. If you want to travel to Paris and come back the day after tomorrow, you can. You have that freedom. Dining out, going to museums and the theatre. Here everything is on debit, and Brazil was the opposite, it was everything on credit; I paid for everything a month later. So I'm still a bit afraid with this financial issue too, which is a huge issue, but it is not the main thing for me now, because it depends whether I can get a good job position in the market over there, I think I can make some money to keep myself well; I can pay my rent, buy a car to travel to the lakes region, understand? Go to the theatre, cinema and restaurants. But several things are coming together. Let's see how it goes, we'll see [Aline].

Thus, Aline continued to lead her life in London, always keeping in mind the idea of returning and living one day at a time, without making many plans.

Just as happened with Aline, when Max got a quieter life with a steady job, he felt himself falling into boredom, especially due to not having many friends in London. Even though he lived in a house with Bernardo and other Brazilians, he spent his time locked in his room. He didn't trust the Brazilians who lived with him and did not create any close relationships with them. He isolated himself inside his bedroom, where he had everything he needed. There was a projector. which he used to screen on the wall images from TV and from his computer. He also had a fridge, a rice cooker, cutlery, and a table. In addition, there was a powerful stereo that he switched on when he had drinks with Jessica - his current girlfriend, whom he met in 2010[34] - and they made their own party in his room.

> It sucks man, I'm very lonely here. In 2009 I had you and we worked together, went out and had fun. But after you went away I had no friend and until I met Jessica, Dude, I was virtually alone. It was just work, home, home, work, I went out with one, I went out with another, I went out with a girl, I went out with another, but never went steady with anyone. So it is like this; you come home every night and put your head on the pillow, and it hits you, and you say: "Man, what am I doing with my life? And also it is hard to meet someone here, because most people who come here, come to party, women who just want to have fun, women who are, let's say, daddy's girl, whose father kept a tight hold on her until the last hair on her head in Brazi;, they come here to get away, you know? They want to have a free life, hang out with as many guys as possible, because when they go back home, the father is going to lock them up again in her bedroom. And to find Brazilian friends is difficult, because one way or another, most people say, even the priest (from the church he is now attending with Jessica) says that many Brazilians want to take advantage of you in some way. So you cannot trust them. I don't have a friend here who I can vouch for, someone I can be sure that he will not fuck me up." [Max].

Thus, due to this negative image that people have about their Brazilian compatriots living in London, Max isolated himself and felt very lonely. Things improved when he met Jessica, but she was not sure whether she wanted to be in London any longer. As such, they even considered getting married so that she would get a visa and stay.

Max, however, came into conflict. He never warmed to the idea of returning to Brazil overnight, even though he felt very lonely in London.

34 Jessica is from São Paulo. She is ten years younger than Max, graduated in International Relations, and went to London to learn English. As it happens with most Brazilians who go to study English, she also became enchanted with life in London and, after a year of living there, she renewed her visa for some more time. It was when she got a job in DS, met Max and they began dating.

The lifestyle acquired through London, marked by consumption and a life without violence, was still a major benefit for him. He was also afraid of making the same mistake as when he returned before, because of memories regarding his ex-wife and his later regrets.

> This is the problem; when I grow within the company, there is this business of going away. When I grew within another company, I became a manager, my ex-wife made me go away. I left because of her. Now I'm pretty much in the same situation, I'm nearly going away because of Jessica. I wish to God that I am not making the same mistake. But it's also the same thing again; I'm going with an open heart, hoping that things will work out in Brazil. In the same way when I came here in 2007. But before I go, I still want to buy some things for my computer, improve it, because I'm leaving. I also want to buy some photographic products and DJ stereos [Max].

Max planned to return to Brazil in March 2011, once again because of another person. He had doubts; sometimes he said that he did not know if it would work out or not, whether he could handle life in Brazil, while at other times he was excited. He said he had several prospects of work with a friend of his, or his brother. However, he just knew he would return to Brazil without having made plans for what to do over there.

Max found himself again redefining his purpose in life and returning to Brazil now because of his girlfriend. But, as he said himself, he didn't plan for the future anymore, he lived his life one day at a time, and if things did not work out in Brazil, he still had his Portuguese document facilitating a return to Europe. He left in August 2011.

In December of the same year I talked to him. He had been in Brazil for four months and he still hadn't found a job that would guarantee the lifestyle he wanted. He sent his resume to several employment agency sites and he had had some interviews but couldn't find the job he wanted. He said that while he was in London, he had heard much talk that Brazil was economically improving, but when he arrived in Brazil, he realized that the country had improved for those who were not working before. There is work, but it pays very little and the cost of living is very high, much higher than "Europe in crisis," as he said. Max could no longer adapt to the lifestyle that he led in Brazil and he was again thinking of returning to London. To date, he hasn't returned and he is still unsure whether Jessica will go with him or not.

In almost all of these cases the perception may be found that loneliness appears as a crushing problem in the lives of migrants who no longer engage with their plans for the future. They live for today without knowing what will happen tomorrow. This situation generates a feeling of insecurity, as well as not belonging, especially in a context where there is a discourse that their countrymen are not trustworthy. In this context of loneliness, churches appear to fill the void that some feel, as happened with Max and Bernardo.

5.1 Loneliness and religion

Jessica was a very religious girl, and as soon as she arrived in London she inserted herself in the existing religious networks of the Catholic Church. She attended Mass every Sunday and also participated actively in prayer groups during the week and other church groups that assisted Brazilians in need of help.

After dating for a month, Jessica and Max were living together, and during this time she began to ask him to attend church with her. Max, who never had a religion until then, began to go to Mass, not feeling very excited initially, but over time it started to fill a void that he had inside himself. Indeed, going to Mass became part of his routine.

> I started going to church because of her (Jessica), because by then, the last time I went to church it was for my wedding in 2002, seven years ago. But I like it. I'm enjoying it. At first I was kind of unsure about going to church, and now I am the one to say to her: "Hey, Sunday, at such time we have to go out, Sunday is the day to go to church." Now for me it is normal to go to Mass on Sundays, it became routine [Max].

Martes (1999) examined the role of churches in the context of migration, when conducting a survey with six Brazilian churches in the city of Massachusetts/USA: three Catholic and three Protestant churches. In her research, she found that all six similarly promoted religious work as well as personal help. In other words, "Brazilian" churches, outside the country had a very strong pastoral role, acting as interpreters and translators in hospitals, schools and before the courts of law. Indeed, they helped to convey information about jobs or housing available, collect and distribute food and clothing, among other types of aid. This situation became clear in the statement of a priest of the church that Max attended, when I questioned him[35] about the role of the "Brazilian" Catholic Church outside Brazil.

> Well, the Catholic Church has always had two dimensions in history: the spiritual and pastoral; even in the ancient church you will get the "Deacon", he wears the stole diagonally, my stole is worn horizontally, that of the "Deacon" is diagonal because he was the man who had the money, he bought the bread to give to the poor. So here it is a mission that has a different job from Brazil, but it has to follow the spiritual; I cannot lose these two dimensions, the spiritual and pastoral. So, while I have to give support, an incentive to put the person back on their feet, even despite the climate of discouragement, unemployment and such, I have to have this pastoral part. Because one thing is connected to the other, there is no way to unlink them. So the church, with successes and errors, it tries to do this and here this help situation is much more real. Maybe in Brazil, it is less because we have the poor people of that street and the church attends that family, and so on, but it is located; here it isn't [Priest].

Being aware of this, the priest during Masses was clearly positioned as a father to all, seeking to provide to the community spiritual support that most sought there. I admit that I was surprised with the way that Mass was conducted. It seemed like a "cult" of evangelical churches that I had visited in Brazil; the priest knew the names of everyone, he talked with people during Mass, calling everyone by name. After the reading of the gospel, he gave the examples from the everyday life of a migrant to illustrate the word of God. In addition, following the end of Mass, he invited people who were there for the first time to go to the front of

35 I went to church with Max and Jessica, conducting an interview with the priest; as well as interviews with church members, besides attending mass.

Picture taken in one of the interviewees home in a small corner of the house.

the altar and introduce themselves, tell everyone where they came from, how long they had been in London, and whether they had already succeeded in finding a job.

Like Martes who saw a paternalistic stance in evangelical pastors in Massachusetts, so it happened with that Catholic Church in London. This was one of the factors that made Max continue going to church.

> Man, I like this priest. He is really a good guy. The other day we came to Mass here and another priest came in, he had come from Brazil, and he came to say a Mass here. I said "Huh? Where's the other? Oh no, I like the other Priest better! I want the other Priest back." I do because he knows more about our reality here. So you identify with him more. You feel more comfortable. He knows the problems we have here; he knows what we go through, and what we don't. He knows what the tricks are... And he does visit a lot of people in jail and such [Max].

As migration often involves feeling a sense of loss and helplessness, many begin attending church to have a space where they find protection and socialization. Thus, the helpless becomes the target audience (MARTES, 1999).

Additionally to coffee time, many who went to Mass also attended church groups during the week. Indeed, these groups aimed to maintain this "intense" community bond. Jessica, for example, participated in two different groups. I remember one day after Mass, the people responsible for these groups informed everyone that there would be a party the following Saturday, to celebrate Saint Valentine's Day. On this occasion, the organizers invited everyone to celebrate Saint Valentine's Day with their respective partners, and those who were not married should also take the opportunity to go and find a trustworthy companion, a fellow believer.

In addition to this role of the church, as a place that provides "spiritual" security and protection, there is also the role of material aid, as it has been described: the act of solidarity. The priest explained that he and another priest from another community divide the functions of "practical" aid. He was responsible for providing support to people who are arrested and have trouble with the police. The other priest was responsible for finding them jobs and medical aid. However, he said that this division was happening naturally, because he also helped in finding jobs for people. Moreover, I saw this happen. At the end of the Mass the priest announced that the churchgoers had passed him some work contacts and people who needed them should go and talk to him soon afterwards.

When I talked to the priest, I asked if people often went there and offered work without wanting anything in return. He replied that there have been many cases of people who didn't pass the information on for free, as they were not sympathetic and wanted to earn some money for it. However, he fought against this practice of selling employment leads[36].

The same day that I had this conversation with the priest (it was interesting because I talked to him before the celebration of Mass), by coincidence I heard, while attending Mass, the Liturgy of the Word – the part of the Mass when the Word of God is read to the faithful – was about solidarity. It was a reading from the Book of the Prophet Isaiah (Isaiah 58.7 -10). And I shall set out this the reading below to make the point:

> "Thus says the Lord: Share the bread with the hungry, and that you bring to your house the poor and pilgrims. When you see the naked, that you cover him, and not hide yourself from your own flesh. Then light shall break forth as the morning, and your health shall spring forth speedily, and the righteousness shall go before you; and the glory of the Lord shall be your reward. Then you will call upon the name of the Lord and He will answer your call, you will ask for help, and he shall say: 'Here I am', if you destroy your instruments of oppression, and leave the authoritarian habits, and language, if you welcome the poor with an open heart, and give all the relief to the needy, your light will rise in the darkness, and your obscure life will be as noon " [Brochure of the Mass's text delivered to the faithful].

Afterwards the priest mentioned the issue of making money by exploiting the needy, those who "sell" information about work to those who needed help. They try to make money by exploiting the ones who already possess nothing. This lack of solidarity was considered as something negative in the church. Other churches didn't always deal with the matter in the same way.

36 In churches in Massachusetts, Martes also witnessed a similar situation, when a priest fought the sale of jobs trying to control the transfer of information through a list he created, in which the work was passed on according to the order of registration. Sales (1999b) also witnessed a campaign in an attempt to end this practice of selling non-Christian jobs in the parish of San Tarcisio in Boston/USA.

Interestingly, Martes' research touches upon this custom of selling jobs. According to her, while Catholic priests condemn the lack of solidarity, some pastors of Protestant churches are now more flexible and sometimes even encourage this sale. This happens, according to Martes, due to the fact that evangelical churches hold a discourse and a religious practice of exhortation to work and actively encourage socio-economic improvement. This appreciation of economic improvement was also recorded in a church that Bernardo started attending.

I once went out at night with Max, Jessica and Bernardo. We went to a pub that was in the neighbourhood where they lived. When we got there, we saw a group of Brazilians sitting together on a couch. As there were some girls, Bernardo approached them to talk. Everyone in that group attended an evangelical church and they had just left a service of communion. Bernardo became interested in one girl, but as she said they only went out with churchgoers, he began to frequent it. Bernardo said that he went there just to win the girl. Initially, what he saw corresponded to his ideas about churches: they spoke only of going to work, earning money and helping the church. Over time, however, he began to feel it also had a positive side: they all helped each other and knew his name, which made him feel like part of something.

> I arrived at the church the first time and there were two guys receiving those arriving. The guy turned around and said, "It's your first day here?" I said, "Yeah. So, I met some girls and they told me to come here." They gave me a paper and told me to enter. The minute I opened the door, everyone looked at me. I remained cool. I stayed at the back, very quiet. The girls asked me to sit with them, I went and I was sharing the Bible with them, and the pastor kept an eye on us. Until then it was ok, the guy spoke only of money, work and even one moment the pastor turned around and said: "Oh, I did not come today with my Mercedes." And the people: "Oh". "I also did not come by bus." And the people: "Oh". "I also did not come by train." "But I also did not get here flying." Everyone: "Hahaha"! The guy was good; he was entertaining everyone telling the story there... He said: "I came walking from home to here, and you know how many of those pennies you throw away, that you hate to carry around, I saved? I saved more than £1.00.

> So from today on you will deposit your pennies in that jar at the entry because we are going to renovate our church." Then I said: "Ah I knew it, the deal here is only money. " But then he started calling everyone by name, telling people's problems, and say that they have a program there called "Feeding something" and every week they help people in need. Dude, they help you from the moment you arrive here, they give you everything, home, work, food, even documents maybe they get too. And after the end of the service he called me up front, called me by my name now, because I had filled a paper in the beginning. He called me there, he made everyone look at me and thank me for being there. After, on other days, I get there and there is a snack bar that sells drumsticks and such, I go down there and people come, call me by my name, thank me for being there and hug me. At first I became frightened because the pastor turned and said, "Give me a hug, Bernardo?" And I said; "Okay." Then everyone comes and hugs you when they see you [Bernardo].

Although having gone initially to church because of the interest in the girl, and then having realized that they only talked about working and giving money to the church, Bernardo still said he felt good about going there, because people called him by his name and hugged him and demonstrated interest in him as a person. Moreover, the fact that the church helped everyone get ahead was also something that made him feel good.

Thus, both in the case of Bernardo and Max, we can see that some Brazilians in London, as well as those studied by Martes, in Massachusetts, USA, seek the church at a time of loneliness, wanting an environment of safety, security and trust, where they can socialize. As a consequence, this religious choice itself is explained by the connections of friends and family, rather than by the tenets of each church (MARTES, 1999).

When I attended church, I remembered that at the hour of prayer, people read from a newsletter that contained the organized acts of Mass. I had done catechism when I was ten years old and I still remembered the prayers, I didn't need to read the newsletter. As many people there were young, I believed that most of them didn't attend church in Brazil. They were like Max; they started attending church in London, seeking to fill this feeling of loneliness. I only interviewed a few people who attended that church, so this is not something that can be said at a general level, but the few I talked to had gone to church from a similar situation to that of Max, to seek a place of safety, security and trust in a context marked by insecurity and lack of solidarity.

For Martes, it is within this context that churches are gaining strength. Since the Brazilian community has a negative view of itself, is barely brotherly and highly competitive. Hence, churches appear as safe and supportive places. Those Brazilians who are there are seen as reliable[37]. This is especially so because the church is an environment that reproduces social control, and it is in these environments that trust and solidarity have more chances to reproduce.

When I asked the priest about this lack of trust among Brazilians, he also said that not only is there a prevalent idea that Brazilians have bad character, there is also a distinction made between the Brazilians in London by regional difference. This tended to decrease within the church, but outside the distinction remained.

> So this is interesting. People make too many generalizations. There are those who say: "Oh, I do not want contact with Brazilians, no. But it is a very small number who disappoint us, we cannot generalize. Like, I'll speak ill of Muslims. There is a neighborhood that is all Muslim and there is the one who throws garbage on the street, There is, of course, the one who insults me if he sees as clergy. Priest Flavio, you did not know him, he got beaten up there in the street, from Muslims; he was wearing a cassock. Now I cannot generalize. The people from the Northeast, they are not all that... right? And the people from São Paulo, *Paulistas*, they are not all hard workers. It isn't like that, so it is therefore a lie. But there is this bias here, yes, but I think here within the community, because of the groups that we have, because of the community and friendship that we have, this bias is decreasing. But it still exists on the

37 In Massachusetts, the Brazilians also have a negative view of Brazilians who live there. There is a discourse of constant low level of trust and solidarity.

> streets. The prejudice against Goiás and Minas Gerais, especially, is very strong here [Priest].

It is interesting to see how this idea of the "*Goiano*", as the one who becomes the "inferior" Brazilian gains strength among Brazilians, and the idea ends up being internalized by all, albeit minimally. During that same conversation, minutes before discussing the issue of prejudice, the priest had made a joke saying that the "*goianada*" (the people from Goiás) had given him peace at the beginning of the year, because they did not need his help in jail.

CHAPTER 6

"BRAZILIANS IN LONDON REVISITED"

As it has already been demonstrated in the first part of this book, the profile of Brazilians migrating to London is similar to that of individuals who migrate to other developed countries. They are theoretically qualified, and in London, they perform functions, which they wouldn't usually perform in Brazil. People work eighty hours a week without any form of social protection; workers use drugs to keep stimulated due to getting paid by the hour, thus allowing them to work more and earn more; some young people apply to be 'guinea pigs' in tests for pharmaceutical companies and are paid to use new medicines, provided they assume full responsibility for any possible damage to their health: workers who, given their undocumented status, are forced to subject themselves to all kinds of work. In other words, they do not fall outside the image of the typical migrant worker who, in search of work, travels the world undertaking labour-intensive and poorly paid work, helping to constantly reproduce the economic inequalities existing at the global level.

However, my own fieldwork, understanding the lives of Brazilian migrants in London as well my own experience as a migrant worker, led me to question my initial theoretical framework. As is the case with many of us, I always had in my imagination an idea about a migrant as the poor worker who migrates to a richer place in search of better conditions of employment. Therefore, when initially carrying out a literature review on global migration, I placed my research within the framework of the economic migrant. Surprisingly, my experiences as a migrant, along with my research findings from fieldwork, pointed to something that went far beyond the sole issue of employment.

As much as these Brazilians have left a 'developing' country, migrating to a 'developed' country, carrying out the various types of work considered as 'un-qualified', largely reserved for migrants, there are different "types" of Brazilians performing these jobs, and in this case, serve to maintain different lifestyles which are constantly being negotiated and redefined. Their reasons for migrating are not the same, and cannot always be 'pigeon-holed' as an economic issue, because reasons such as family dynamics, gender and class, for instance, are directly linked to migration processes, both in relation to the reasons that led the individual to migrate, as to how each individual migratory path is evolved. Alongside with this economic desire there aare other reasons such as: increased access to material and symbolic products and good public services, fleeing family pressure, new forms of sociability and life experience, and a desire to see the world. These were also reasons that made many migrants re-negotiate their migration project.

Meanwhile, when analysing the lives of these migrants and the way they conduct their everyday lives in the host society, it is also possible to see the inequalities that constitute the uneven global world being expressed by such displacement. These inequalities can be seen from the very beginning of their journey, whey they present their reasons to migrate, since their social and economic differences intertwine to define the level of their desire/desperation/need to leave their country. These, together with other differences, such as being either a documented or undocumented migrant, will also affect how these migrants enter and live in the new host society and the level of mobility available to them.

Social networks are, in fact, the main element of attraction and support for these migrants in the host country. Most received help from friends/relatives to undertake the migration process and to adapt in their host society. Social contact is the main source of information in finding a job; yet, due to their undocumented status, many end up being exploited in London by their own compatriots. Some 'employers' use this 'ethnic network' to pay undocumented workers less than the minimum wage and make them perform extensive hours of heavy work, with constant threats of denunciation. A similar situation happens to the majority of migrants by their own ethnic networks in the host society, such as the case of Koreans, Bolivians, Jews, Syrians and Lebanese in Brazil (Truzzi and Sacomano Neto, 2007).

Having said that - just like Knowles and Harper (2009) noted in their work with English and Filipino migrants in Hong Kong - in a world in motion it is not enough to know that people move from one place to another throughout social networks which help them in the migration process; it is also necessary to notice how these migrants live these mobile journeys, with long and short durations, in their daily lives and to pay attention to how these social ties are used and negotiated by them in everyday practices.

As demonstrated repeatedly in this work, it is not always the principle of solidarity that directs and guides these social ties. Often there is, somehow, a rational calculation at the time an individual introduces another into a network. There is an expectation that the appointed, or indicated, person will correspond to the requirements needed to be part of that "network". When the expectations of the person appointed are fulfilled, the one who appointed him or her also obtains symbolic gains and prestige. Furthermore, in several cases, the principle of trust which unites all the members of the network, also functions as a form of social control: the person must have self-control at all times, so as not to break the trust of the network. In the case of companies, specifically, managers use this self-control in their day-to-day work.

Thus, the network functions not only as a factor of integration but also of control and exclusion, since those who have already been inserted once and have broken trust do not "socially exist" any longer, in practice, for those they had related to previously.

Another interesting point is that there is a constant process of reflection and revaluation about life goals, which these migrants go through. This marks their lives with a permanent temporariness and fluidity. When analysing the trajectories of Max, Guilherme and Bernardo, who are people who theoretically would fit into the idea of the "economic migrant", we could note that after a period in London, these migrants began to reshape their daily practices in a way that would call into question the neatness of that theoretical idea. In many cases, the initial goal of migrating to work and save money lost central importance in their lives and other personal needs were highlighted, making that initial intention of returning soon lose its centrality in their lives. Consequently, the question of the temporal nature of their situation gained substantial weight. Many reported that most Brazilians saw themselves coming to London short-term, particularly because they were only able to obtain temporary visas. Yet, the vast majority of these temporary workers ended up staying longer than anticipated, without knowing for sure when they would return to Brazil. They stopped trying to plan for the future, living each day one at a time, limiting their social and emotional investments, since a temporary and transitional life consists of social connections which are not deeply constituted (Knowles, 2003). Not surprisingly, many – such as Aline, Priscila, Guilherme and Max - complained of loneliness and the difficulty of making "real friends" as the major problem of living in London.

As migration studies show, this constant negotiation of life goals and the existence of a flexible life without many plans for the future, make the distinction quite vague between temporary and "permanent" migrants. Margolis (1994) in his study of Brazilians in New York, for example, shows that the idea of the return was always present not only among those with a clear intention to work for a stipulated period, but also among those whose estimated time had elapsed and had achieved their planned goals.

Picture taken in one of the interviewees kitchens whilst they were cleaning.

In other words, the migrant is constantly reformulating their migration project and, as much as the idea of returning is something always present in their discourses, nevertheless many of them purchase goods which are more reflective of settling down than of returning to Brazil. As in the case of Aline who bought furniture despite saying she would be leaving soon, or Priscila paying a lawyer to secure another five years in England despite saying she did not want to stay in London for more than one year. This is the moment when the process of settlement starts.

Sales (1999b) when working with Brazilians in Boston found a similar situation and stated that these individuals undergo a process of redefining their life project, since they initially migrated intending to leave after a short period of time. They ended up redefining their situation and began working with the prospect of staying in the U.S. longer, but always keeping clearly in mind the idea of returning. As stated by Sayad (1998), the return is an essential element of the migrant even though he will never actually return. Knowles and Harper (2003) also place the idea of returning as a feature of migrant life. Staying longer means being permanently ready to leave. In other words, keeping alive the ever-present notion of the return is also a way of staying.

Therefore, as the cases presented in this book demonstrate, Brazilians in London are also in a constant process of negotiation and reconstruction of their goals. Performing a micro-analysis, specially by tracing the trajectories of those who would have fit the "ideal type" of the work migrant, marked by the triad of migration-save money-return, it was possible to notice that this reappraisal of goals and lifestyles is something present in various trajectories. This would not be possible to witness using a macro perspective, in which the migrant is solely a subject looking for better working conditions. Likewise, it is an oversimplification to characterize them as simply students or workers, as these categories are too loose when their trajectories are analysed. According to the data presented, students may come to have a lifestyle focused on work and workers can later have the "lifestyle" of a student.

Another interesting point to consider here is the question of dedication and eagerness to work, especially in the early years of the migration project, a fact that makes these "migrant bodies" turn into simple "commodities", regardless of the reasons given to migrate. Whether aiming to save money and invest in Brazil, or use money earned to renew a visa, these migrants who migrated for different reasons and had different lifestyles, initially all participated in this logic of 'work hard, play hard', which allowed them to earn as much money as they could as well as enjoying their chosen lifestyle to the extreme. This happened even with those who had no previous intention to work hard in order to save money, as was my case and that of the three women presented in this book.

Once inserted into the new space, these individuals incorporate the logic of their migrant group as a form of social interaction, where hard work is one of the factors that compose it. Other factors are the short-sighted idea of a life of consumption, mobility, easy access to goods (material and symbolic) and services (such as good quality public services) new forms of sociability, the so-called life experience or the desire "to see the world". These and other aspects make up this group's variety of responses when questioned about the reason why they are in London (cf. EVANS *et al.*, 2010; Cwerner, 2002).

It is fascinating to note that, even though the issue of class, gender, race and social capital may present differentials, both at the point of entry and during the stay of these individuals in this new location (see early chapters), there is an intersection of experiences that pervade all newly arrived migrants who perform unskilled jobs (FRANGELLA, 2010). The "work hard", in order to maintain the lifestyle that they choose to live, is one of these early experiences shared by all. Thus, especially during the first year of the migration project, there is a very strong enchantment with the lifestyle in London; "working hard" is part of the set of social values and logic in this new form of sociability that these individuals start to experience at the beginning. When I got sick, for example, after a few months working without a break I started to reflect on the issue of temporary and casual work that I performed in London, and how my body was nothing more than a mere commodity. When I was working in London, I could make some comparisons between my work and the one developed by prostitutes albeit in relative terms. Of course, when making the comparison here is the element value-judgment about the way they work, as well as the actual way that their bodies are used. However, if these two issues are left aside, it all boils down to a similar situation: the use of one body by another, within a given time, with a pre-stipulated worth. And, most likely, with time these bodies will no longer serve the purpose for those who have contracted it. It is exactly at this point that the initial dedication to working hard begins to decrease, since one's body can no longer withstand the effort.

In relation to the "intra-community" coexistence, based on my experience, I realized that the 'winner's culture' is a constituent part of the one who migrates and this must at all times maintain a certain status among two distinct groups: those with whom they coexist in London and with those who stayed in Brazil. Among the first group, the status and distinction comes through consumption, the work that is carried out and the foreigners with whom they relate. As for the second group, since they are separated spatially, social networks act as a window to give that "visibility to successful life" through the posting of travel photos, goods purchased and frequency in nightclubs.

In addition to my main observations, it became apparent from conversations with migrants that at first there seems to be a sense of belonging and integration between these workers. Newcomers are always amazed when they hear Brazilians speaking Portuguese on the streets and are proud to say they are Brazilian. Yet, as time goes on, the great majority change their discourse and begin to have a negative image of their fellow Brazilian migrant, impacting the formation of their identities in London.

The creation of social boundaries amongst Brazilians was secondary in my analysis, which appeared in the latter part of my fieldwork. Based on the analysis of conflicts and speeches, I could see that in Brazil there is a structure of pre-established domination, in which "each has its place", and the situations and social positions seem to be naturalized because of the length of time that these are reproduced throughout history. When Brazilians leave the country to lead life as an migrant, they start at least initially to coexist with fellow nationals. In order words, white and middle-class Brazilians begin to coexist with blacks, *Baianos* (people from Bahia), *Goianos* and *Paraíbas* (people from Paraíba) with the same social status, if not lower. This is more so when people with identities representing "stigma" in Brazil, now hold higher positions at work in London. This happens because, for Englishmen, all migrants are best understood within "racialized boundaries", no matter where they are from in Brazil –whether they are *Paulistas* or *Cariocas* (São Paulo or Rio) -, and consider themselves white. In such cases of "migrant work", one of the main attributes that relate to a higher hierarchical level achieved by their occupational position is the knowledge of the local language (FUSCO, 2007) and not race, for example.

Consequently, a black woman, a *Paraiba*, who has been in the country longer, and speaks the local language, has more chance of a higher position than a *Carioca* newcomer who does not speak the language. In this instance, as said by Priscila, "blacks think they are people", because a black person in Brazil has and "knows" their place of invisible subordination. On the other hand, while in London, among their peers they are 'people' who are visible, bothering those who were not accustomed to being submissive, as in the case of Rose, and to be subordinate to blacks, *Baianos* and *Paribas*.

It is at this point of contrast and "the breaking of hierarchy" that prejudice and discrimination come to the fore, in which the discourse of a racial democracy which exists in Brazil ceases to be valid. At this moment the hierarchy is broken, and must be reinforced by those who previously held a hegemonic position. For such, it seems like individuals begin to make use of identity markers, or categories of articulation - race, ethnicity, gender, class (PISCITELI, 2008) constructed according to the Brazilian social reality, as a way to rebuild this hierarchy.

These markers are not in isolation from one another; these categories exist in and through the relationships between them and they are articulated or intersected categories (BRAH, 2006; MCKLINTOCK, 1992, 1995; PISCITELI, 2008). However, according to the context of interaction, a given social marker (for example race) may become the main source to produce difference and establish racialized boundaries. It is also important to emphasize that 'difference' does not always refer to inequality and discrimination, but in certain contexts these identity markers can be used as a means of 'ranking' a relationship.

Therefore, it was possible to see how these Brazilians "manipulate" their multiple identities (HALL, 2006)[38] as a way to differentiate themselves within a new context, especially when a hierarchy is broken. After all, even close social relationships negotiate hierarchies and small differentiations (KNOWLES and HARPER, 2009).At a micro level these individuals are at various times negotiating and manipulating different identity markers as a way to rank and distinguish themselves in a rela-

38 For Hall, the rapid economic, cultural and political changes that modified the capitalist societies changed from the 60s - and intensified in the 80s and 90s with the technological revolutions - also changed the configuration of the subject itself, emerging in now what Hall calls the postmodern subject, consisting of multiple identities that this subject starts to resort to in a "game of identities", even though they may be contradictory.

tionship. The identities will function more as a symbolic capital to create these divisions within the interaction; these categories - race, ethnicity, gender, - belong to the symbolic order and are created and given a new meaning within the interaction. Thus, these symbols are flexible and can be manipulated to establish "upper" and "lower" divisions according to the frame reference (MARTES, 2003).

In a context of migration these conflicts become more evident, because, as stated by Knowles and Harper (2009), migration circulates to the operating surface of race and ethnicity in the world, and in a new social context these categories recombine with others that are also important for thinking and categorizing subjects, such as nationality, class, age and gender. They gain new forms and meanings in new contexts, their differences are exposed through proximity: individuals who migrate settle in new places with bodily features and social practices of their country of origin, which all take on new forms and meanings in the receiving society.

Although race, class and ethnicity are not objects in themselves, concepts about them can be implemented as an array of objects, as they are ways of thinking, categorizing, and organizing people who make the "difference", to include some and exclude others, providing gains for some and creating barriers for others.

This is a situation that deserves more attention in research on Brazilian emigration and social differentiation in transnational studies. Although this had not been the main focus of my research, this notion was something that appeared constantly during my everyday life in London amongst Brazilians working in unskilled jobs. Drawing upon the research, it would be interesting to analyse how social differences are translated and re-made from Brazil to a new social context. Further work should also take into account those who don't perform the so called "migrant jobs", who didn't appear in this work but nevertheless constitute a significant population in London. Brazilians in London are not a homogenous group; they belong to different classes and are in the U.K for different reasons. Thus understanding how social differences are translated and can result in new forms of racialized and other boundaries amongst the given group, can provide a better way to comprehend transnational flows connecting the local to the global in everyday life.

References

AUGUSTÍN, L., La industria del sexo, los migrantes y la família europea, **Cadernos Pagu** nº25, julho-dezembro, 2005.

ASSIS, G. **Estar aqui, estar lá...uma cartografia da vida em dois lugares**. Florianópolis, SC. Dissertação de Mestrado em Antropologia - Programa de Pós- Graduação em Antropologia Social, UFSC. 1995.

_________. Estar Aqui, Estar Lá ... uma cartografia da vida entre o Brasil e os Estados Unidos - **Campinas: Núcleo de Estudos de População/UNICAMP**, jun.2002.

_________. De Criciúma para o mundo: os novos fluxos da população brasileira: gênero e rearranjos familiares. In: MARTES, A. C B., FLEISCHER, S. (Orgs.) **Fronteiras cruzadas:** etnicidade, gênero e redes sociais. São Paulo: Paz e Terra, 2003. p. 199-230

ASSIS, G.; CAMPOS, E; SIQUEIRA, S. As redes sociais na configuração da migração internacional para os Estados Unidos. In: **34 anual da ANPOCS, 2010, Caxambu (MG). anais do 34 anual da ANPOCS.** São Paulo : Editora ANPOCS, 2010. v. 1. p. 1-25.

ASSUNÇÃO, V. K. . Brasileiros em Boston: as mudanças no cenário da oferta de alimentos e o fluxo transnacional de produtos nas redes sociais. In: **34 Encontro Anual da ANPOCS, 2010**, Caxambu. Anais do 34 Encontro Anual da ANPOCS, 2010.

ALMEIDA, J.; MIRANDA, M. O uso de pronomes de primeira pessoa em artigos acadêmicos: uma abordagem baseada em corpus. Veredas – **Revista de Estudos Lingüísticos**, v. 13, n. 2, p. 68-83, 2009.

ALVES, M. **Como escrever teses e monografias** - um roteiro passo a passo. Rio de Janeiro: Elsevier, 2007.

BAUMAN, Z. **Modernidade líquida**. Rio de Janeiro: Jorge Zahar, 2001.

_______________ **Globalização:** as conseqüências humanas. Rio de Janeiro: Jorge Zahar, 1999.

BECK, U; GIDDENS, A.; LASH, S. ***Modernização Reflexiva**: política, tradição e estética na ordem social moderna.* Oeiras: Celta Editora, 2000.

Benson, M ; O'Reilly, K., Lifestyle Migration: Expectations, Aspirations and Experiences. Surrey: Ashgate, (2009)

_______________ **Globalização:** as conseqüências humanas. Rio de Janeiro: Jorge Zahar,
1999.

BOLTANSKI, L. ; CHIAPELLO, È. **O novo espírito do capitalismo.** São Paulo: Martins Fontes, 2009.

BOURDIEU, P. **A Distinção:** crítica social do julgamento, Porto Alegre, Editora Zouk, 2007.

BRAH, A. Diferença, Diversidade, Diferenciação. In: **Cadernos Pagu**. Campinas: Núcleo de Estudos de Gênero Pagu, 2006.
BRIGGS, X. Bridging networks, social capital and racial segregation. In **America. Cambridge:** KSG Faculty Research Working Paper Series, 2003.

CWERNER, S. 2002 The times of migration. **Journal of Ethnic and Migration Studies**, 27(1): 7-36- 2002.

CASTLES, S.; MILLER, M. J. **The age of migration:** international population movements in the modern world. Palgrave MacMilliam, New York, 2003

CLASTRES, P. Da tortura nas sociedades primitivas. In: **A sociedade contra o Estado**. 5ª. ed. Rio de Janeiro: Francisco Alves, 1990.

COSTA, F. B. **Homens Invisíveis:** Relatos de uma humilhação social. São Paulo: Globo, 2004.

DA MATTA, R. **Casa & rua:** espaço, cidadania, mulher e morte no Brasil. 5 ed. Rio de Janeiro: Rocco, 1997.

DELEUZE, G. **Conversações:** 1972-1990. Rio de Janeiro: Ed. 34, 1992.

DE CERTEAU, M. **A invenção do cotidiano**. Petrópolis: vozes, 1994.

DIAS, G. T. Casa de brasileiros em Londres: a importância da casa para os imigrantes brasileiros" In. **Travessia- Revista do Migrante** – Publicação do CEM – Ano XXIII, no66, Janeiro-Junho, 2010.

________________________. **O processo de fixação do migrante brasileiro em Londres:** a importância das práticas cotidianas na elaboração de sua identidade. Ponto Urbe, no 3, versão 4.0, julho de 2009.

DURHAM, E.R. **A caminho da cidade:** a vida rural e a migração para São Paulo. 3° ed. São Paulo: Perspectiva, 1984.

ELIAS, N; SCOTSON, J. **Os estabelecidos e os Outsiders:** sociologia das relações de poder a partir de uma pequena comunidade. Rio de Janeiro: WVA, 2000.

EVANS, Y. WILLS, J. DATTA, K. HERBERT, J. McILWAINE, C. MAY. J. ARAÚJO, J.O. FRANÇA, A.C. FRANÇA, A.P. **Brasileiros em Londres:** relatório para a campanha De Estrangeiros a Cidadãos, London: Department of Geography, Queen Mary, University of London, 2007

FERNANDES, D. M. e RIGOTTI, J. I. R. Os Brasileiros na Europa: notas introdutórias. Texto apresentado no **Seminário "Brasileiros no Mundo"**, realizado em 17 e 18 de julho no Palácio do Itamarati, Rio de Janeiro, 2008.

FLEISCHER, S. R. **Passando a América a limpo:** o trabalho de housecleaners brasileiras em Boston, Massachusets. S.Paulo, Annablume, 2002.

FRANGELLA, S. O Made in Brasil em Londres: migração e os bens culturais. In. **Travessia- Revista do Migrante** – Publicação do CEM – Ano XXIII, no66, Janeiro-Junho, 2010.

FREYRE, G. **Sobrados e mucambos**. São Paulo-SP: Editora Global, 2003.

FOCOSI, R. M. **Caminhoneiros: trabalho precário e comportamento de risco**. Trabalho de Conclusão de Curso. (Graduação em Ciências Sociais) - Universidade Federal de São Carlos, 2009.

FUSCO, W. ,Redes Sociais na Migração Internacional: o caso de Governador Valadares. In: **Textos Nepo**, Unicamp, n. 40. Campinas. 2002.

___________. Capital Social e Dinâmica Migratória: um estudo sobre brasileiros nos Estados Unidos. **Textos Nepo,** Unicamp, v. 52, Campinas, 2007.

Giddens, **A. The Consequences of Modernity**. Stanford University Press, California, 1990.

GOZA, F. A imigração brasileira para a América do Norte. **Revista Brasileira de estudos de população**. v.9 n.1 jan./jul. 1992.

GOZA, F. Redes sociais e a integração de brasileiros no Canadá e nos Estados Unidos. In: Ana Cristina Braga Martes and Soraya Fleischer (Orgs.) **Fronteiras cruzadas:** etnicidade, gênero e redes sociais. São Paulo: Paz e Terra. 2003, p.263-288.

GRANOVETTER, M. Ação Econômica e estrutura social: o problema da imersão. **RAI-eletrônica.**v.6,n.1,art 9, jan/jun. 2007.

HALL, S. **A identidade cultural na pós-modernidade.** Tradução Tomás Tadeu da Silva, Guaracira Lopes Louro. 11. ed. Rio de Janeiro: DP&A, 2006.

HOLANDA, S. B. de. **Raízes do Brasil**. 26a edição. São Paulo, Companhia das Letras, 1995.

KNOWLES, C. **Race and Social Analysis.** London. Sage, 2003.

KNOWELES, C; HARPER, D. **Hong Kong:** Migrant lives, Landscapes, and Journeys. Chicago Press, 2009.

KNOWLES, C; ALEXANDER, C. **Making Race Matter:** bodies, space and identity. Palgrave Macmillan, 2005.

Knowles, C. (2010) Mobile sociology British Journal of Sociology 2010 Special Anniversary Issue.

LAHIRE, B. **Retratos Sociológicos. Disposições e Variações Individuais**. Porto Alegre, Artmed, 2004.

LASCH, C. **O Mínimo Eu:** sobrevivência psíquica em tempos difíceis. São Paulo, Brasiliense, 1990.

LIGHT, I. ; GOLD, S. J. **Ethnic Economies.** San Diego CA: Academic Press, 2000.

LIMA, J. C.; CONSERVA, M. de S. . **Redes sociais e mercado de trabalho:** entre o formal e o informal. Política & Trabalho, João Pessoa, v. 24, p. 73-98, 2006.

LIMA, J. C. ; MOURA, M. C. Trabalho atípico e capital social: os agentes comunitários de saúde na Paraíba. **Sociedade e Estado**, Brasília, v. 20, n. 1, p. 103-133, jan.-abr. 2005

LIMA, J. C ; MARTINS JR, A. Productive Restructuring, Informality, and Mobilities In Latin America: The Case of Bolivians in São Paulo and Brazilians in London". Artigo submetido para publicação, 2012.

MARGOLIS, M. **Little Brazil An Ethnography of Brazilian Migrants in New York City.** Princeton: Princeton University Press, 1994.

___________. Na virada do milênio: a emigração brasileira para os Estados Unidos . In: MARTES, A. C. B.; FLEISCHER, S. (Orgs.). **Fronteiras cruzadas:** etnicidade, gênero e redes sociais. São Paulo: Paz e Terra, 2003,p.51-72.

MARQUES, E. C. . **Redes sociais, segregação e pobreza**. São Paulo: Unesp, 2010.

MARTES, A. C. B. ; FAZITO, D. Economic Sociology - **The European eletronic newsletter**, v. 11, 2010, p. 43-53

MARTES, A. C. B. Os imigrantes brasileiros e as igrejas em Massachusetts. In: REIS, R.; SALES, T. (orgs.). **Cenas do Brasil migrante.** São Paulo: Editora Boitempo, 1999.

_______________. Raça e Etnicidade – Opções e Constrangimentos. In: **Fronteiras Cruzadas:** Etnicidade, Gênero e Redes. Ana Cristina Braga Martes and Soraya Fleischer (eds). Petropolis, RJ, Brazil: Editora Paz e Terra, 2003, p. 73-98.

MACHADO, I. J. R. Implicações da imigração estimulada por redes ilegais de aliciamento: o caso dos brasileiros em Portugal. **Ilha. Revista de Antropologia** (Florianópolis), v. 7, 2005, p. 187-212

MASSEY, D. S.; GOLDRING, L. **Continuities in transnacional migration:** an analysis of thirteen Mexican communities. Washington (Paper presented at Workshop U.S. Immigration research: an assessment of data needs for future research, financed by National Research Council), 1992.

McGOVERN, P. **Immigration, labour markets and employment relations:** problems and prospects. British Journal of industrial relations, 2007

McKLINTOCK, A. **Imperial leather, Race, gender and sexuality in the colonial contest**. Routledge, 1995.

_________________. The Angel of Progress: Pitfalls of the term "pos-colonialism". **Social text**, n. 31/32, Third World and Post-Colonial Issues, p. 84-98, 1992.

MCPHERSON, M., Smith-Lovin, L. e Cook, J. 2001. **Birds of a feather:** homophily in social networks. In: Annual Review of Sociology, No 27

MRE. **Brasileiros no Mundo, Subsecretaria Geral da comunidades brasileiras no exterior**, 2ª edição, 200. Disponível em <www.brasileirosnomundo.mre.gov.br/pt-br/estimativas_populacionais_das_comunidades.xml>, Acesso em 12/10/2010.

NARDI, H. C. A propriedada social como suporte da existência: a crisedo individualismo moderno e os modos de subjetivação contemporâneos. **Psicologia & Sociedade**; 15 (1): 37-56; jan./jun.2003.

NITAHARA SOUZA, Y. A Diáspora Uchinanchu: Uma rede transnacional na era da globalização. **In: 34 Encontro Anual da ANPOCS, 2010**, Caxambu, MG. 34 Encontro Anual da ANPOCS, 2010.

OLIVEIRA, A. C. de. O Caminho sem Volta - Classe social e etnicidade entre os brasileiros na Flórida. In: Ana Cristina Braga Martes; Soraya Fleischer. (Org.). **Fronteiras Cruzadas.** 1 ed. São Paulo: Editora Paz e Terra S/A, v.1, 2003, p. 115-138.

PISCITELLI, A. Interseccionalidade, categorias de articulação e experiências de migrantes brasileiras. **Sociedade e Cultura**, vol.11, nº2, Jul/Dez, 2008

RAUD-MATTEDI, C. Análise crítica da Sociologia Econômica de Mark Granovetter: Os limites de uma leitura domercado em termos de redes e imbricação. **Política e Sociedade**, 6, 2005, p. 59-82

RESENDE, R. Brasileiros no sul da Flórida – Relatos de uma pesquisa em andamento, In Martes, A. C. B. e Fleischer, S., **Fronteiras cruzadas:** etnicidade, gênero e redes sociais, São Paulo, Paz e Terra, PP, 2003

RIBEIRO, G. L. Goiânia, Califórnia: vulnerabilidade, ambigüidade e cidadania transnacional. Brasília, Departamento de Antropologia, Universidade de Brasília. **Serie Antropologia** v.235 1998

SOARES, W. **Emigrantes e investidores:** redefinindo a dinâmica imobiliária na economia valadarenses. Rio de Janeiro. Dissertação [Mestrado - Programa de Pós-Graduação do Instituto de Pesquisa e Planejamento Urbano e Regional, Universidade Federal do Rio de Janeiro, 1995

___________. **Da metáfora à substância:** redes sociais, redes migratórias e migração nacional e internacional em Valadares e Ipatinga. Tese [Doutorado] - Centro de Desenvolvimento e Planejamento Regional, Universidade Federal de Minas Gerais, Belo Horizonte, 2002.

___________. A emigração valadarense à luz dos fundamentos teóricos de análise de redes sociais. In: MARTES, Ana Cristina B.; FLEISCHER, Soraya (Orgs.). **Fronteiras cruzadas: etnicidade, gênero e redes sociais.** São Paulo: Paz e Terra, 2003.

SALES, T. Novos Fluxos da população brasileira. **Revista Brasileira de estudos de população.** São Paulo. v. 8, n 1/2. Jan./dez, 1991.

________. **Brasileiros longe de casa.** São Paulo: Editora Cortez, 1999, 240p.

________. O trabalhador brasileiro no contexto das novas migrações internacionais. In: PATARRA, N.L, BAENINGER, R., MIYASHIRO, A (org.) **Emigração e imigração internacionais no Brasil Contemporâneo.** São Paulo: FNAUAP- Fundo de População das Nações Unidades e ABC – Agência Brasileira de Cooperação, v.1, Editora LTR, 1995, p.89-103

_________. Identitidade Étnica Entre Imigrantes Brasileiros na Região de Boston, EUA In REIS, R. R. & SALES, T. (orgs.). **Cenas do Brasil migrante**, São Paulo, Boitempo, 1999b, pp.15-44.

SASAKI, E. M. **Dekasseguis:** Trabalhadores Migrantes Nipo-Brasileiros no Japão. Campinas: UNICAMP, Núcleo de Estudos de População, 2000.

SASSEN, S. **The mobility of labor and capital.** Cambridge: University Press, 1988.

SAYAD, A. **A Imigração ou Os Paradoxos da Alteridade**. São Paulo: USP, 1998.

SCUDELER, V. C. **Imigrantes valadarenses no mercado de trabalho dos EUA**.Cenas do. Brasil Migrante. Eds. Rossana Rocha Reis and Teresa Sales(org).São Paulo.Boi tempo, 1999

SENNETT, R. **A cultura do novo capitalismo**. Rio de Janeiro: Record, 2006.

___________. **A corrosão do caráter**: conseqüências pessoais do trabalho no novo capitalismo. Rio de Janeiro: Record, 2004.

SIMMEL. G. A Metrópole e a Vida Mental.
In: VELHO, Otávio G (org.). **Fenômeno Urbano**. Ed. Guanabara, Rio de Janeiro, 1987.

TELLES, V. S. Ilegalismos e a cidade. In: **Novos Estudos Cebrap**, *2009, 84: 153-173..*

______________. Nas dobras do legal e ilegal: ilegalismos e jogos de poder nas tramas da cidade. Dilemas, **Revista de Estudos de Conflito e Controle Social**, *2010, p. 97-126.*

TORRESAN, A. **Quem parte, quem fica. Uma Etnografia sobre imigrantes brasileiros em Londres.** *Dissertação de Mestrado apresentada ao Programa de Pós-Graduação em Antropologia Social do Museu Nacional da Universidade Federal do Rio de Janeiro. 1994*

TRUZZI, O. M. S. Redes em processos migratórios. **Tempo Social** (USP. Impresso), v. 20, 2008, p. 199-218

TRUZZI, O. M. S. ; SACOMANO NETO, M. Economia e empreendedorismo étnico: balanço histórico da experiência paulista. RAE. **Revista de Administração de Empresas**, *v. 47, 2007, p. 37-48*

URRY, J. **Mobilities**. *Polity* Press, Malden, United Kingdom, 2008.

VERTOVEC, S. Superdiversity and its implications. In: **Ethnic and Racial Studies**. v. 30, 2006, p. 1024 - 1054.

WACQUANT, L. **Corpo e Alma Notas Etnográficas de um Aprendiz de Boxe**. Rio de Janeiro: Relume Dumará. 2002.

WHYTE, W. F. **Sociedade de esquina**. Rio de Janeiro: Jorge Zahar. 2005.

WOLKOWITZ, C.; WARHURST, C. 'Embodying labour'. In **Working life:** renewing labour process analysis, 223 - 243, Editors: Thompson, P. and Smith, C. Basingstoke: Palgrave Macmillan, 2010.

WEBER, M. Relações comunitárias étnicas. In: **Economia e Sociedade.** Brasília: UnB, v. 1, 1991. p. 267-277.

References

Published

Whyte Tracks
Møllehavevej 11
3200 Helsinge
Denmark - DK33581513